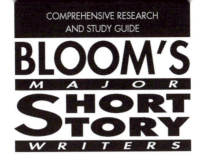

COMPREHENSIVE RESEARCH
AND STUDY GUIDE

BLOOM'S

MAJOR

SHORT STORY

WRITERS

Raymond

Carver

EDITED AND WITH AN
INTRODUCTION BY HAROLD BLOOM

CURRENTLY AVAILABLE

BLOOM'S MAJOR DRAMATISTS

Aeschylus
Aristophanes
Bertold Brecht
Anton Chekhov
Henrik Ibsen
Ben Johnson
Christopher
  Marlowe
Arthur Miller
Eugene O'Neill
Shakespeare's
  Comedies
Shakespeare's
  Histories
Shakespeare's
  Romances
Shakespeare's
  Tragedies
George Bernard
  Shaw
Neil Simon
Oscar Wilde
Tennessee
  Williams
August Wilson

BLOOM'S MAJOR NOVELISTS

Jane Austen
The Brontës
Willa Cather
Stephen Crane
Charles Dickens
William Faulkner
F. Scott Fitzgerald
Nathaniel Hawthorne
Ernest Hemingway
Henry James
James Joyce
D. H. Lawrence
Toni Morrison
John Steinbeck
Stendhal
Leo Tolstoy
Mark Twain
Alice Walker
Edith Wharton
Virginia Woolf

BLOOM'S MAJOR POETS

Maya Angelou
Elizabeth Bishop
William Blake
Gwendolyn Brooks
Robert Browning
Geoffrey Chaucer
Sameul Taylor
  Coleridge
Dante
Emily Dickinson
John Donne
H.D.
T. S. Eliot
Robert Frost
Seamus Heaney
Homer
Langston Hughes
John Keats
John Milton
Sylvia Plath
Edgar Allan Poe
Poets of World War I
Shakespeare's Poems
  & Sonnets
Percy Shelley
Alfred, Lord
  Tennyson
Walt Whitman
William Carlos Williams
William Wordsworth
William Butler Yeats

BLOOM'S MAJOR SHORT STORY WRITERS

Jorge Louis Borges
Italo Calvino
Raymond Carver
Anton Chekhov
Joseph Conrad
Stephen Crane
William Faulkner
F. Scott Fitzgerald
Nathaniel Hawthorne
Ernest Hemingway
O. Henry
Shirley Jackson
Henry James
James Joyce
Franz Kafka
D.H. Lawrence
Jack London
Thomas Mann
Herman Melville
Flannery O'Connor
Edgar Allan Poe
Katherine Anne Porter
J. D. Salinger
John Steinbeck
Mark Twain
John Updike
Eudora Welty

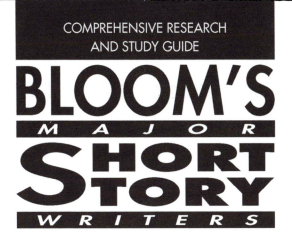

COMPREHENSIVE RESEARCH
AND STUDY GUIDE

BLOOM'S
MAJOR
SHORT STORY
WRITERS

Raymond
Carver

EDITED AND WITH AN INTRODUCTION BY HAROLD BLOOM

First Printing
1 3 5 7 9 8 6 4 2

Library of Congress Cataloging-in-Publication Data
Raymond Carver : edited and with an introduction / by Harold Bloom.
    p. cm. — (Bloom's major short story writers)
    Includes bibliographical references and index.
    ISBN 0-7910-6821-8
    1. Carver, Raymond—Criticism and interpretation. 2. Carver,
Raymond. I. Bloom, Harold. II. Series..
    PS3553 .A7894 Z84 2002
    813'.54—dc21   2002000604

Chelsea House Publishers
1974 Sproul Road, Suite 400
Broomall, PA 19008-0914

www.chelseahouse.com

Contributing Editor: Aaron Tillman

Layout by EJB Publishing Services

DEC 2 2009

CONTENTS

USER'S GUIDE

This volume is designed to present biographical, critical, and bibliographical information on the author and the author's best-known or most important short stories. Following Harold Bloom's editor's note and introduction is a concise biography of the author that discusses major life events and important literary accomplishments. A plot summary of each story follows, tracing significant themes, patterns, and motifs in the work. An annotated list of characters supplies brief information on the main characters in each story. As with any study guide, it is recommended that the reader read the story beforehand, and have a copy of the story being discussed available for quick reference.

A selection of critical extracts, derived from previously published material, follows each character list. In most cases, these extracts represent the best analysis available from a number of leading critics. Because these extracts are derived from previously published material, they will include the original notations and references when available. Each extract is cited, and readers are encouraged to check the original publication as they continue their research. A bibliography of the author's writings, a list of additional books and articles on the author and their work, and an index of themes and ideas conclude the volume.

ABOUT THE EDITOR

Harold Bloom is Sterling Professor of the Humanities at Yale University and Henry W. and Albert A. Berg Professor of English at the New York University Graduate School. He is the author of over 20 books, and the editor of more than 30 anthologies of literary criticism.

Professor Bloom's works include *Shelly's Mythmaking* (1959), *The Visionary Company* (1961), *Blake's Apocalypse* (1963), *Yeats* (1970), *A Map of Misreading* (1975), *Kabbalah and Criticism* (1975), *Agon: Toward a Theory of Revisionism* (1982), *The American Religion* (1992), *The Western Canon* (1994), and *Omens of Millennium: The Gnosis of Angels, Dreams, and Resurrection* (1996). *The Anxiety of Influence* (1973) sets forth Professor Bloom's provocative theory of the literary relationships between the great writers and their predecessors. His most recent books include *Shakespeare: The Invention of the Human*, a 1998 National Book Award finalist, *How to Read and Why* (2000), and *Stories and Poems for Extremely Intelligent Children of All Ages* (2001).

Professor Bloom earned his Ph.D. from Yale University in 1955 and has served on the Yale faculty since then. He is a 1985 MacArthur Foundation Award recipient and served as the Charles Eliot Norton Professor of Poetry at Harvard University in 1987–88. In 1999 he was awarded the prestigious American Academy of Arts and Letters Gold Medal for Criticism. Professor Bloom is the editor of several other Chelsea House series in literary criticism, including BLOOM'S MAJOR SHORT STORY WRITERS, BLOOM'S MAJOR NOVELISTS, BLOOM'S MAJOR DRAMATISTS, MODERN CRITICAL INTERPRETATIONS, MODERN CRITICAL VIEWS, and BLOOM'S BIOCRITIQUES.

EDITOR'S NOTE

My Introduction centers upon "Cathedral," one of Carver's best-known stories, which seems to me shadowed by D.H. Lawrence's mode of story-writing, an unacknowledged but perhaps beneficent influence upon the later Carver.

"Where I'm Calling From" is studied by its critics as a fable of what Claudine Verley calls "interiority" and Kirk Nesset names as "insularity." In their different ways, Adam Meyer, Thomas J. Haslam, and Michael Sonkowsky also touch on the radical solipsism that attends both alcoholism and its continuities.

"Cathedral" touchingly is praised by Irving Howe for its insight into human loneliness, while Mark Facknitz sees it as one of the stories in which Carver apprehends individual value. This kind of desperate humanism is expounded by Arthur Brown, and is adumbrated by Carver's widow, Tess Gallagher, and his friend, Tom Jenks. A dissent is recorded by Melvin Jules Bukiet, for whom the empathy developed in "Cathedral" still seems rather minimal.

"Fever" is praised for its reconcilements to reality in essentially similar terms by Michael Bugeja, Arthur Salzman, Randolph Paul Runyan, and Ewing Campbell.

"The Bridle," a story of exemplary and controlled pathos, is seen as another breakthrough by James Grinnel, Patricia Schnapp, and Ewing Campbell, all of whom emphasize the contrast between narrative sympathy and inarticulate characters.

"What We Talk About When We Talk About Love" is seen by M.B. Gentry and W.L. Stull as a great effort that depleted Carver. That struggle to get beyond the "minimalist label" is also depicted, from varying perspectives, by Nelson Hathcock, Michael Trussler, Jon Powell, and Brian Stonehill. The televisional aesthetic of channel surfing is related by Bill Mullen to a salient feature of Carver's final style.

INTRODUCTION

Harold Bloom

I have an imperfect sympathy for Raymond Carver's stories, though I agree with such eminent critics as Frank Kermode and Irving Howe that Carver was a master within the limits he imposed upon himself. So overwhelming was Hemingway's influence upon Carver's earlier stories that the later writer wisely fended Hemingway off by an *askesis* that went well beyond the elliptical style practised by the author of *The First Forty-Nine Stories*. In his own, final phase, Carver began to develop beyond an art so largely reliant upon leaving things out. "Cathedral" is my favorite story by Carver, but it involves the fully aware reader in some perplexity, because of its puzzling relationship to D.H. Lawrence's magnificent short story, "The Blind Man." It seems hardly possible that Carver did not know how much "Cathedral" owed to "The Blind Man," but literary influence is a labyrinth, and good writers can become remarkably schooled at repression, or unconsciously purposeful forgetting.

Keith Cushman first noted Carver's debt, which Cushman wittily termed "blind intertextuality." In Lawrence's story, the visiting friend who comes from afar can see; it is the husband who is blind. Carver's story is based upon a visit from a blind friend of Tess Gallagher's, and ends with an overcoming of the narrator's jealousy of the visitor:

> So we kept on with it. His fingers rode my fingers as my hand went over the paper. It was like nothing else in my life up to now.
> Then he said, "I think that's it. I think you got it," he said. "Take a look. What do you think?"
> But I had my eyes closed. I thought I'd keep them that way for a little longer. I thought it was something I ought to do.
> "Well?" he said. "Are you looking?"
> My eyes were still closed. I was in my house. I knew that. But I didn't feel like I was inside anything.
> "It's really something," I said.

This poignant opening to otherness is overmatched by the parallel passage in Lawrence, when the blind husband establishes contact with the terrified visitor:

"Your head seems tender, as if you were young," Maurice repeated.

"So do your hands. Touch my eyes, will you? –touch my scar."

Now Bertie quivered with revulsion. Yet he was under the power of the blind man, as if hypnotised. He lifted his hand, and laid the fingers on the scar, on the scarred eyes. Maurice suddenly covered them with his own hand, pressed the fingers of the other man upon his disfigured eye-sockets, trembling in every fibre, and rocking slightly, slowly, from side to side. He remained thus for a minute or more, whilst Bertie stood as if in a swoon, unconscious, imprisoned.

Then suddenly Maurice removed the hand of the other man from his brow, and stood holding it in his own.

"Oh, my God," he said, "we shall know each other now, shan't we? We shall know each other now."

Bertie could not answer. He gazed mute and terror-struck, overcome by his own weakness. He knew he could not answer. He had an unreasonable fear, lest the other man should suddenly destroy him. Whereas Maurice was actually filled with hot, poignant love, the passion of friendship. Perhaps it was this very passion of friendship which Bertie shrank from most.

"We're all right together now, aren't we?" said Maurice. "It's all right now, as long as we live, so far as we're concerned."

"Yes," said Bertie, trying by any means to escape.

This is scarcely a comparison that Carver can sustain, but then Lawrence is extraordinary in his short stories, fully the peer of Turgenev, Chekhov, Joyce, Isaac Babel, and Hemingway. Carver, whom perhaps we have overpraised, died before he could realize the larger possibilities of his art. In "The Blind Man" there is a homo-erotic element, but it is secondary. Blind Maurice is admitting Bertie to the interiority that is shared only with his wife, but Bertie cannot bear intimacy: he has been seared by the touch. There is a reverberation in Lawrence's story that carries us into the high madness of great art. Carver, though a very fine artist, cannot carry us there.

Raymond Carver

Raymond Carver was born in Clatskanie, Oregon on May 25, 1938, to Clevie Raymond and Ella Casey Carver. In 1941, Raymond's family moved to Yakima, Washington where Raymond's only sibling, James Carver, was born.

On June 7, 1957, Carver married his sixteen-year-old girlfriend, Maryann Burk. Their first daughter, Christine LaRae, was born later that year. The following year, Carver and his in-laws moved to Paradise California, where he attended Chico State College as a part-time student. His son, Vance Lindsay, was born on October 17th of that year. In 1959, Carver and his family moved to Chico California where he took a creative writing class with John Gardner. In 1960, he founded and edited the first issue of the Chico State literary magazine *Selection,* before he transfered to Humbolt State College. Then in 1961, his story "The Furious Seasons," was published in *Selection,* No. 2.

In 1962, "Pastoral" was accepted for publication in the *Western Humanities Review.* The following year, he received his A.B. degree from Humbolt State. Later that year, he accepted a $500 fellowship for a years's graduate study at the Iowa Writers' Workshop, but he left before the academic year was through. In 1964, his short story "Will You Please Be Quiet, Please?" was published in the journal *December,* and later anthologized in *The Best American Short Stories 1967.*

In the spring of 1968, Raymond Carver's first book, *Near Klamath* (poems), was published by the English Club of Sacramento State College. In 1970, another collection of poems, *Winter Insomnia*, was published by Kayak Press. Later that year he received the National Endowment for the Arts Discovery Award for Poetry, and his short story "Sixty Acres" was included in *The Best Little Magazine Fiction, 1970.* In 1971, Gordon Lish, fiction editor at *Esquire*, published Raymond's short story "Neighbors." That same year, Raymond was appointed visiting lecturer in creative writing at the University of Santa Cruz, for 1971-72.

Raymond received a Wallace E. Stegner Fellowship at Stanford University for 1973-1974. During this time, he received the Joseph

Henry Jackson Award for Fiction, and was also lecturing at University of California, Berkeley. In 1973, he served as a visiting lecturer at the Iowa Writers Workshop, where he lived two floors below John Cheever. That same year, Raymond's story "What Is It?" was included in the O. Henry Awards *Prize Stories 1973* and five of his poems were reprinted in *New Voices in American Poetry.*

Put Yourself in My Shoes was published as a Capra Press chapbook in August 1974 and later included in the O. Henry Awards *Prize Stories 1974.* His story "Are You a Doctor?" was included in the O. Henry Awards *Prize Stories 1975.* The following year, Raymond's third book of poetry, *At Night the Salmon Move,* was published, and his first major-press book, the short story collection *Will You Please Be Quiet, Please?* was published by McGraw-Hill. It was also in that same year when his story "So Much Water So Close to Home" was included in the first Pushcart Prize Anthology.

In 1977, Raymond was awarded a Guggenheim Fellowship, and his first collection of stories, *Will You Please Be Quiet, Please?* was nominated for a National Book Award. He published yet another collection of stories *Furious Seasons and Other Stories,* that year, and while attending a writers' conference in Dallas, Texas he met poet Tess Gallagher. The following year, he was the Visiting Distinguished Writer at the University of Texas at El Paso, and in 1979, he received a National Endowment for the Arts Fellowship for Fiction.

In 1980, Raymond started teaching at the University of Syracuse, and he and Tess Gallagher purchased a house together. The following year, the short story collection *What We Talk About When We Talk About Love* was published by Knopf and edited by Gordon Lish—the title story was included in the *Pushcart Prize Anthology.* In 1982, he and Maryann Carver got divorced. Later that year, "Cathedral" was included in *Best American Short Stories* and the *Pushcart Prize Anthology.*

In 1983, *Cathedral* was published by Knopf, and "Where I'm Calling From," was included in *Best American Short Stories.* Later that year, "A Small, Good Thing" was reprinted in O. Henry Awards *Prize Stories 1983* and the *Pushcart Prize,* and *Cathedral* was nominated for both the National Book Critics Circle Award and the Pulitzer Prize. *Fires: Essays, Poems, Stories* was also published that year, and he received a Mildred and Harold Strauss Living Award which provided a stipend that allowed him to resign his from his post at Syracuse University.

In 1984, his collection of poems *If It Please You* was published, and his short story "Careful" was selected for a *Pushcart Prize.* The following year, another collection of poems *Where Water Comes Together With Other Water* was published by Random House, and *This Water* was published by Ewert. That same year, he was award-ed the Levinson Prize, *Dostoevsky: A Screenplay,* which he wrote with Tess Gallagher, was published by Capra Press, and *The Stories of Raymond Carver* was published by Picador Press.

In 1986, Carver served as guest editor of *The Best American Short Stories 1986,* and Random House published his poetry collection *Ultramarine.* The following year, *American Short Story Masterpieces,* which he edited with Tom Jenks, was published by Delacorte. Also that year, his final short story, "Errand," was printed in *The New Yorker* and "Boxes" was included in *The Best American Short Stories 1987.*

It was in 1987 when Carver experienced pulmonary hemorrhag-es, leading to the removal of two-thirds of his cancerous left lung. The following year, "Errand" received first place in *Prize Stories 1988,* and it was also included in *The Best American Short Stories 1988.* In March of 1988, his cancer reappeared in his brain. While he was undergoing intensive radiation treatments, his collection of new and selected stories *Where I'm Calling From* was published. On June 17 of that year, he and Tess Gallagher were married in Reno, Nevada. At 6:20 am on August 2, Raymond Carver died of cancer in his house in Port Angeles, Washington. The following year, Atlantic Monthly Press published his final collection of poems *A New Path to the Waterfall.*

"Where I'm Calling From"

"Where I'm Calling From," the title story to Raymond Carver's penultimate collection of short stories—originally published in the collection *Cathedral*—opens on the front porch of Frank Martin's "drying-out facility," where the first person narrator is talking to a fellow resident named J.P. The narrator, whose name is never revealed, informs the reader that J.P. is an alcoholic who makes his living as a chimney sweep. This is J.P.'s first time at Frank Martin's facility. He is younger than the narrator who happens to be at Frank Martin's for the second time.

J.P. is gripped by the shakes and the narrator, who can sympathize, assures him that they will eventually calm down. Meanwhile, the narrator is concerned about a recurring twitch that occurs in his shoulder and neck. He is particularly concerned today after witnessing one of the residents, Tiny, fall into a seizure. The reader is told that Tiny is an electrician from Santa Rosa who was meant to go home in a couple of days, in time to spend New Years with his wife. On the day of his seizure, he was seated at the head of the breakfast table, amusing the other residents with an animated story about duck hunting. Tiny starts talking about one of his drinking bouts when suddenly he's on the floor, gripped in the throws of a seizure. "So every time this little flutter starts up," the narrator says, speaking of the pinch in his shoulder, "I draw some breath and wait to find myself on my back, looking up, somebody's fingers in my mouth."

Still sitting on the porch before lunch, J.P. continues to tell stories of his younger days. He starts with a story of when he was a boy, and he fell into a well. He speaks about the fear and anxiety he felt before his father came by and pulled him back up. At the narrator's urging, J.P. tells another story, this one about his wife. He was only a year or two out of high school at the time, and he was at a friend's house drinking beer. Before long, the woman hired to clean the chimney and the fireplace arrived and J.P.'s friend let her in. While she was working, J.P. and his friend drank beer and watched the female chimney sweep work. When she was finished, she asked

J.P.'s friend if he would like a kiss, claiming that it was good luck. J.P. asked if he could also have one too, and she agreed.

After accepting a kiss on the lips, J.P. followed the chimney sweep outside to her car where he helped her load some materials into the truck, after which he asked her out on a date. The woman's name is Roxy and after that day, J.P. started joining her on some of her jobs. As time went on, they began dating more seriously and eventually they decided to marry—making J.P. one of the partners in Roxy's father's business. When Roxy became pregnant, J.P. started drinking.

When J.P. first started drinking, he only drank beer. It wasn't until later that he switched to gin and tonic and his life began spinning out of control. He and Roxy got into some fights after that, one leading Roxy to break her husband's nose. As J.P. notes, "He returned the favor." Though Roxy's brother and father threatened to beat him up, J.P. could not stop himself from drinking. Eventually Roxy found herself another man, and J.P. lost his head, cutting her wedding ring into pieces with a wire cutter. Then he got arrested on a "drunk charge" and couldn't go to work. Finally Roxy's brother-in-law and father-in-law dragged him into Frank Martin's and left him there to get his life back in order.

While J.P. and the narrator are on the porch, Frank Martin comes out and tells a story about the novelist Jack London who had lived nearby and died from alcohol. Frank suggests that the narrator and J.P read *The Call of the Wild.* "It's about this animal that's half dog and half wolf. End of sermon."

The narrator takes this opportunity to provide some background information stating that the first time he came to Frank Martin's he came with his wife. This time however, he came with his girlfriend, and they were both drunk on champagne. He thinks about his girl-friend's "mouthy teenaged son," and how he had moved in with them after his wife made him leave the house. He says he feels sorry for his girlfriend, mostly because "on the day before Christmas her Pap smear came back, and the news was not cheery." It was news like that that justified their drinking, which is what they did starting that evening and continuing straight through Christmas Day. They drank bourbon and ate little more than salted nuts. Finally, the narrator decided that he had had enough. Though on their way out to Frank

Martin's where the narrator was planning to dry out, they bought champagne at a package store and drank it all the way there. Then he realizes that he hasn't spoken with his girlfriend since he checked in. He assumes that she made the trip back safely, and acknowledges that he will inevitably see her again as it was his car she drove home in. Finally the dinner bell clangs and he and J.P. head inside.

On the morning of New Years Eve, the narrator calls his wife but there is no answer. He still has things at her house. But instead of getting himself worked up about it, he turns his thoughts to another guy at Frank Martin's who travels a lot. This man claims to have his drinking under control, despite not remembering how he arrived.

The narrative resumes on New Years Eve, at Frank Martin's celebratory steak dinner. The narrator's appetite is starting to return and he finishes everything on his plate with ease. But Tiny, who was supposed to be home in time for New Years, barely touches his food. The narrator asks for his portion and Tiny slides it to him without a word.

After dinner, while everyone is watching the New Years broadcast from Times Square, Frank Martin brings out a cake. J.P. eats two slices and lights up a cigarette. His hands have stopped shaking. He says that his wife is coming to visit in the morning. The narrator acknowledges the hopeful news and before bed, decides to call his own wife, but again there is no answer. He then tries his girlfriend, but hangs up before it rings, realizing that he doesn't really want to talk to her, particularly if there is something wrong.

The following morning, while the narrator and J.P. are out on the porch, J.P.'s wife Roxy arrives. The narrator shakes her hand after they are introduced and says that J.P. has told him a lot about her. Roxy kisses her husband on the cheek and asks if J.P. mentioned that he was the best chimney sweep in the business. Just before J.P. and Roxy head inside, the narrator asks for a kiss. J.P. looks down, seemingly embarrassed, and Roxy says that she's no longer a chimney sweep. But then she agrees to kiss him anyway, planting one on his lips.

When J.P. and Roxy head inside, the narrator is left alone on the porch, his hands trembling with the urge for a drink. He calms himself by thinking about a house that he and his wife had lived in earlier in their lives. He remembers a Sunday morning when he had heard a noise outside. He went to check it out and discovered that his landlord was painting the house. The landlord acknowledged him with a grin and a thumb to the sun. As the narrator continued to watch, he suddenly realized he was naked.

Following this reflection, he thinks about calling his wife again. He also thinks about calling his girlfriend, but does not want to speak with her son. Then he thinks about Jack London and wonders if he's read any books by him. He is reminded of a story he read in high school about a guy in the Yukon who tried to prevent himself from freezing to death by building a fire. This guy finally got one going but then something happened and it died out. Following this reflection, he decides to call his wife, vowing not to start a fight or talk about false resolutions. He also decides to call his girlfriend, hoping only that her son won't answer.

"Where I'm Calling From"

The Narrator, never named, is checked into Frank Martin's rehabilitation center for the second time, again for alcohol. He is separated from his wife, and had been living with his girlfriend before he decided to dry out. He spends most of the story on the porch, talking to another resident named J.P. who is at Frank Martin's for the first time.

J.P. (Joe Penny) was brought to Frank Martin's by his father-in-law and brother-in-law after several unfortunate altercations with his wife, Roxy. J.P. works as a chimney sweep for Roxy's father's company, and although he is good at his job, his drinking becomes unmanageable. He spends most of the story on the porch, talking about his life to the narrator, who encourages him to talk.

Roxy is J.P.'s wife. She shows up at the end of the story and agrees to give the narrator a kiss for luck—a chimney sweep tradition.

Frank Martin owns and runs the rehabilitation center. He tells J.P. and the narrator a story about the novelist Jack London who also had a problem with alcohol.

Tiny is another resident at Frank Martin's. He was supposed to return home before New Years, but he had a seizure and stayed on.

CRITICAL VIEWS ON

"Where I'm Calling From"

ADAM MEYER ON THE EVOLUTION OF RAYMOND
CARVER'S MINIMALISM

[Adam Meyer is an essayist and a scholar whose work has
appeared in such journals as *Critique: Studies in
Contemporary Fiction.* In this excerpt, Meyer speaks on
Carver's final movement out of minimalism, seen most
notably in his penultimate collection *Where I'm Calling
From.*]

At this point in his career, there can be little doubt that Raymond
Carver is "as successful as a short story writer in America can be,"
that "he is becoming an Influence." Still, despite (or perhaps because
of) this position, Carver remains a controversial figure. Much of the
debate about Carver's merits centers around a similar debate about
minimalism, a style that a few years ago was very hot and very hotly
criticized, and that, now that it is cooling off, is under even more fer-
vent attack. Much of the controversy is sparked by a confusion of
terminology. As hard as it is accurately to define minimalism, for the
same reasons we cannot entirely pin down such terms as realism,
modernism, or post-modernism. It is even harder to say who is or is
not a minimalist, as demonstrated by Donald Barthelme's being
called a minimalist as often as he is called one of the post-mod-
ernists against whom the minimalists are rebelling. Nevertheless,
Carver is generally acknowledged to be "the chief practitioner of
what's been called 'American minimalism.'" Now that this has
become a pejorative appellation, however, his admirers are quickly
trying "to abduct [him] from the camp of the minimalists." If he is
to be successfully "abducted," however, it will not be because the
label is no longer popular, but because it no longer fits.

   The fact of Carver's membership in the minimalist fraternity has
never been fully established. Many critics, as well as Carver himself,
noted that his latest volume of new stories; Cathedral, seemed to be
moving away from minimalist writing, that it showed a widening of

perception and style. This is certainly true, but it is not the whole story. If we look back over Carver's entire output, an overview encouraged by the recent publication of his "selected" stories, *Where I'm Calling From*, we see that his career, rather than following an inverted pyramid pattern, has actually taken on the shape of an hourglass, beginning wide, then narrowing, and then widening out again. In other words, to answer the question "Is Raymond Carver a minimalist?" we must also consider the question "Which Raymond Carver are we talking about?," for he did not start out as a minimalist, and he is one no longer, although he was one for a period of time in between.

> —Adam Meyer, "Now You See Him, Now You Don't, Now You Do Again: The Evolution of Raymond Carver's Minimalism," *Critique: Studies in Contemporary Fiction*, Vol. 30, No. 4 (Summer 1989): pp. 239-240.

CLAUDINE VERLEY ON THE HIDDEN DEPTH OF THE STORY

[Claudine Verley is a critic and a literary scholar whose work has appeared in such journals as *Short Stories for Students* and *Journal of the Short Story in English.* In this excerpt, Verley discusses the hidden depth contained in the story.]

"Where I'm Calling From" can be read in the following way: two alcoholics meet up in a rehabilitation centre, one of them tells his life story while the other—the narrator—listens and is then reminded of some of his own personal adventures. Life in the centre on December 31st is briefly portrayed and the narrator is trying in vain to telephone his wife while his friend, J.P., is actually visited by his wife, Roxy, the following day. The narrator's name remains a mystery as do any personal details, except for the fact that he is separated from his wife while at the same time he is not particularly interested in his girlfriend. He is afraid of having a heart attack and has clearly not recovered from his addictive state. This is all and it is not a great deal.

Only by making an implicit comparison between J.P. and the narrator can such a narrative, which is as bare of actual events as many other of Carver's works, form any consistent unity. However we cannot grasp the richness of it if we limit ourselves to declaring that Roxy has no equivalent life-force in the narrator's existence since he remains alone at the end. We are plunged into a melodrama of alcoholism and conjugal life if we remain on the surface of things, with the dullness of the present and the pitiful shallowness of the lives depicted. Carver could thus be described as a minimalist or a miniaturist and the critics who use these terms are not paying homage to his talent by doing so.

On the contrary I would like to suggest that there is a true depth to be found in Carver's work but not in those areas where it is usually sought: neither in a psychological complexity nor in the polysemy of the themes, nor even in the intricacies of a rich style. Carver's interiority is not so much described as staged and the depth is produced by the different layers of the retrospections, the overlapping of the focalisations, the alternating and sometimes even the blending of the voices and finally the use of techniques which allow both for the diversification of narrative sources and the extension of tenses far beyond their traditional uses.

The story which I have chosen to analyse here provides a good example of this hidden depth.

—Claudine Verley, "Narration and Interiority in Raymond Carver's 'Where I'm Calling From,'" *Journal of the Short Story in English*, No. 13 (Autumn, 1989): pp. 91-102.

THOMAS J. HASLAM ON THE DIFFERENCES BETWEEN
TWO VERSIONS OF THE STORY

[Thomas J. Haslam is an essayist and a scholar whose work has appeared in such journals as *Studies in Short Fiction* and *Short Stories for Students*. In this excerpt, Haslam speaks on the evolution of the story and the difference between the version that was first printed in *The New Yorker* and the final version that came out in Carver's penultimate collection *Where I'm Calling From*.]

Raymond Carver liked to revise his stories. He won critical acclaim from reviewers and academics alike for rewriting "The Bath" from What We Talk About When We Talk About Love (1981) into "A Small, Good Thing" for Cathedral (1983); and he published in Fires (1984) a selection of revised stories as well as an essay on his practice. It is hardly surprising that there are three published versions of Carver's "Where I'm Calling From." The story initially appeared in the New Yorker (15 March 1982); it was significantly revised for Carver's highly praised Cathedral; and, with a few slight changes, was reprinted in his new and collected stories, Where I'm Calling From(1989). There are substantial differences between the first and last published versions of the story. These revisions—not all of which are improvements—are also a sort of commentary, providing both new matter and means for a critical appreciation of "Where I'm Calling From." Reading both story versions for their strengths and weaknesses, I comment on five key differences between New Yorker text and the Where I'm Calling From text. In doing so, I hope to foreground (and later argue for) Carver's understanding of people as intrinsic story-tellers, as dialogic selves who find their meaning, value and identity through and by interaction with other selves, other stories. Of course, the textual findings I present are better understood as illustrating rather than proving my basic claim about Carver and the narrative self.

The first difference between the two story versions concerns the narrator's description of a rival for his girlfriend's attention and affection. The New Yorker text reads:

> She tried to explain to her son that she was going to be gone that afternoon and evening, and he'd have to get his own dinner. But right as we were going out the door this Goddamned kid screamed at us. He screamed, "You call this love? The hell with you both! I hope you never come back. I hope you kill yourselves!" Imagine this kid!

The revised Where I'm Calling From text reads:

> She tried to explain to her kid that she was going to be gone for a while and he'd have to get his own food. But right as we were going out the door, this mouthy kid screamed at us. He screamed, "The hell with you both! I hope you never come back. I hope you kill yourselves!" Imagine this kid!

The final version is less blatant, but subtlety is not the highest virtue. In favor of the New Yorker text, the "Goddamned" Oedipal "son" carries more weight than the revised gender-neutral "mouthy kid"; and positioned as the narrator's male rival, the teenaged son provides both a moral and practical reference lacking from the revised version. His parting shot—"You call this love? To hell with you both"—condemns his mother and the narrator for their bleak, clearly dysfunctional relationship centered on alcohol abuse, careless—rather than casual—sex, and a shared indifference that seems more like mutual contempt. In favor of the final version, however, the changes from "that afternoon and evening" to "a while" and from "dinner" to "food" brilliantly underscore the chaotic and harmful aspects of the lovers' relationship: the kid is left to fend for himself—and not just miss dinner—for an indefinite period as his mother disappears with her boyfriend into the void.

—Thomas J. Haslam, "'Where I'm Calling From': A Textual and Critical Study," *Studies in Short Fiction*, Vol. 29, No. 1 (Winter, 1992): pp. 57-64.

KIRK NESSET ON THE DEPTH OF THE STORY

[Kirk Nesset has been a professor of English and Writer-in-Residence at Whittier College. He is a novelist, short story writer, poet and essayist. He is the author of *The Stories of Raymond Carver: A Critical Study*. His essays have appeared in such journals as *American Literature* and *Profils Americins*. In this excerpt, Nesset discusses the hidden depth contained in the story.]

"Where I'm Calling From" is the story of a man coming to grips with addiction within the security of an alcohol treatment home. Contrary to the situations of "The Compartment," "Preservation," and "Careful"—situations in which men blockade themselves in ways as offensive to others as they are self-destructive—this narrator's confinement is both positive and necessary. Locking himself up voluntarily in "Frank Martin's drying out facility" (127), he is a stronger version of Wes in "Chefs House," a wavering recoveree who lapses back into alcoholism when his summer retreat—the sanctuary of his fragile recovery—falls out from under him. Up until now, this narrator (like many of Carver's narrators, he goes unnamed) has insulated himself with drink, with the buffering torpor alcohol can provide, his addiction being both a reaction to and the cause of his failing marriage. Arriving at Frank Martin's dead drunk, exchanging one extreme state of insularity for another, he takes refuge from a prior refuge—one that was killing him. Sitting on the porch with another recovering drunk, J.P., he takes further refuge in the story his new friend has to tell.

It is significant that throughout most of the story Carver leaves his characters sitting where they are. Protected yet still exposed to the chill of the outer world, the porch is that liminal space existing between the internal security of a cure-in-progress and the lure, if not the danger, of the outer world. On the porch, the narrator and J.P. are at once sheltered and vulnerable, their physical surroundings an objective correlative to the transitional state of their minds and wills. Beyond the "green hill" they see from the porch, as Frank Martin tells them, is Jack London's house—the place where the famous author lived until "alcohol killed him" (137). Beyond that—much farther north—is the "Yukon," the fictive topos of London's "To Build a Fire," a place where, as the narrator recalls later, a man will "actually . . . freeze to death if he can't get a fire going" (146). With his wet clothes, tragically enough, London's figure is hardly insulated from the chill, even though, ironically, he's bundled up in the manner of the two strongest figures in Carver's story: J.P.'s wife, Roxy, whose "big knuckles" have broken her husband's nose, wears both a "coat" and "a heavy sweater" (142); Frank Martin, hard-edged and tough and looking like a "prizefighter," keeps his "sweater buttoned all the way up" (137).

By the end of the story, sitting alone and enjoying the transitional comforts of the porch, Carver's narrator fails to recall, or subconsciously omits, the tale's sad conclusion—the fact that, at the mercy of the elements, London's man eventually freezes to death, his life extinguished along with his fire. Still upset perhaps about Tiny's "seizure," the narrator chooses not to think of the extreme consequences of ill-prepared exposure to the outer world. Nor does he remind himself that death entered the heart of the sanctuary only days before, this time without claiming its prize. Subject also to bodily complaints, J.P. suffers from the "shakes" and the narrator from an occasional "jerk in [his] shoulder"; like Tiny, the fat electrician from Santa Rosa, J.P. and his friend are each in their own way over-powered by biology, by nature. Their bodies—like their minds—are adjusting and compensating in the process of recovery. Just as love was once upon a time "something that was out of [J.P.'s] hands"—something that set his "legs atremble" and filled him "with sensations that were carrying him every which way" (132)—the aftermath of drinking is for both men superseded in intensity only by death, the ultimate spasm, which proceeds from both within and without, insulate themselves however they may.

—Kirk Nesset, "Narration and Interiority in Raymond Carver's 'Where I'm Calling From,'" *The Stories of Raymond Carver: A Critical Study* (Athens: Ohio University Press, 1995): pp. 57-58.

MICHAEL SONKOWSKY ON GROWN MEN IN "WHERE I'M CALLING FROM"

[Michael Sonkowsky has taught college English and written on a wide range of topics in education. He was involved in the development of an alternative educational program designed to take an intergenerational approach to learning. In this excerpt, Sonkowsky discusses the growth of the male characters in the story.]

The stories in Raymond Carver's 1983 Cathedral collection include possibilities for characters' growth and development not found in his earlier stories. Carver commented in interviews that he was aware of something "totally different" about the stories as he was writing them—something which, as he put it, "reflects a change in my life." Reflections of two of the biggest changes in the author's life—quitting drinking in 1977 and sharing a home with writer Tess Gallagher since 1979—can certainly be found in "Where I'm Calling From." The story concerns an alcoholic narrator who befriends a fellow alcoholic named J.P. at a treatment center they have both checked into. Much of the hope for change in the lives of the two main characters seems to lie in establishing better relations with women: at the story's end, J.P. is embraced by his wife and the narrator resolves to call his wife and his girlfriend.

For the most part, however, women in "Where I'm Calling From" remain off stage. The story's setting, "Frank Martin's drying out facility," is a decidedly male place. "Just about everyone at Frank Martin's has nicks on his face," as the narrator points out, from shaving. A key to understanding the characters' potential for growth lies in the images of helpful—or potentially helpful—older men that appear throughout the story. Carver presents a series of interactions between males of different ages that depict personal transformations in various ways and seem to hint at the importance of father-like figures.

J.P. begins his communication with the narrator by sharing a boyhood memory of falling down a dry well and being rescued by his father. The most vivid aspect of the memory seems to be the fear and sense of isolation J.P. experiences looking up from where he landed: "In short, everything about his life was different for him at the bottom of that well." It is easy to imagine that J.P.'s reminiscence has been triggered by the parallels between the bottom of that well and his current situation—isolated from loved ones, in another "dry" place, after having "hit bottom," looking out at a midday sky from the porch. The memory of being rescued by his father, then, comes as a kind of infantile wish, a fantasy of the personal transformation which both J.P. and the narrator want to undergo.

J.P. is brought to Frank Martin's at a point when he has started falling again—falling off roofs while drunk at work. It is interesting to note that he is handed over to Frank Martin's care by male escorts, his father-in-law and brother-in-law, and that "the old guy signed him in." Frank Martin, however, proves to be a much less nurturing substitute father. The proprietor of this treatment facility for men exhibits exaggerated masculine characteristics: he is physically large, smokes cigars, and stands "like a prizefighter." In an abrupt "sermon," he advises J.P. and the narrator to consider the famous writer Jack London, who, though "a better man than any of us," died of alcoholism. The "rugged individualist" model of manhood embodied by Jack London's adventure tales—and by the brusque Frank Martin—does seem deadly to J.P. and the narrator, who are more in need of support from others. In J.P.'s childhood memory, his father rescues him from a hole where young J.P. "was thinking of insects"; Frank Martin's effect on J.P. is only to make him "feel like a bug."

—Michael Sonkowsky, "Grown Men in 'Where I'm Calling From,'" *Short Stories for Students* (Gale, 1998).

PLOT SUMMARY OF

"Cathedral"

"Cathedral," the title story to one of Carver's most acclaimed collections, opens with the narrator's concern over a blind friend of his wife's who's coming to spend the night. This blind man's wife had recently passed away and he is visiting her relatives who live in Connecticut. He called the narrator's wife from his in-laws. Though the narrator's wife has kept in touch with him—mailing tapes back and forth—she hasn't seen him in ten years, when she worked for him one summer in Seattle. The narrator is ill at ease about his impending arrival, and the idea of his blindness makes him uncomfortable. He admits that his understanding of the blind comes from movies where they are often portrayed as slow moving and humorless.

Ten years ago, when the narrator's wife worked for this man, she was in dire need of a job. She was engaged to a man who was training to be an officer in the military, and neither of them had any money. She responded to an ad in the paper for someone to read reports and case documents to a blind man. The job also entailed arranging his office in the county social-service department, and by the end of the summer, they had established a significant friendship. With the friendship established, he asked if he could touch her face before she left. She agreed, letting his fingers roam around her face and neck. It was an experience she said she'll never forget. She even wrote a poem about it, something she often did after a significant experience.

This poem about the blind man was one of the first things she shared with the narrator once they started dating. The narrator remembers that the poem was about how she felt as the blind man's fingers were on her face.

But before the narrator met his wife, she had married the officer to whom she had been engaged and began a life as a military wife, constantly moving from place to place. Throughout this entire time, she continued to trade tapes with the blind man. She told him of the poem she had written about him, and how she was writing another poem about what it was like to be an officer's wife. Eventually the loneliness of moving from place to place coupled with the inability to sustain any meaningful friendships, took its toll on her and she tried to end her life by swallowing the pills in her medicine cabinet and sinking into a hot tub. Instead of dying, she vomited all over the bathroom and passed out, only to be found by her husband who called an ambulance in time to save her life. She included all these details on the tape she sent the blind man. As time went on, she told him about her separation with this officer, then her divorce, and then her new relationship with the narrator. She documented all the details of her life on tape and sent them off to the blind man who reciprocated with tapes of his own.

The narrator even heard one of the blind man's tapes. His wife asked if he wanted to listen, so he did. He got some drinks for them and listened to the blind man's recorded message, but he became uneasy at hearing his name come out of this stranger's mouth. And just before the blind man gave his opinion about what he had heard of the narrator, there was a knock on the door and their listening was interrupted. "Maybe it was just as well," the narrator says. "I'd heard all I wanted to."

Clearly uncomfortable about the blind man's arrival, the narrator's wife appeals to him for acceptance, claiming that she would make any friend of his feel comfortable. The narrator responds by saying that he doesn't have any blind friends. His wife counters by saying that the narrator doesn't have any friends, and she reminds him that the blind man's wife has just died. The narrator does not seem capable of compassion.

The narrator's wife explains that Beulah, the blind man's wife, had worked for the blind man, whose name is Robert, the summer after she left. The idea of a blind man married to a woman who might have already developed cancer strikes the narrator as unreal.

When the narrator's wife goes to pick up Robert, the narrator has a drink and watches TV. Upon their return, the narrator looks out the window and is struck by his wife's smile and Robert's full beard. He quickly finishes his drink and greets his wife and guest at the door. He shakes Robert's hand, and Robert says that he feels as if they've already met. The narrator returns the sentiment, not knowing how else to respond.

They all sit down in the living room and the narrator, still consumed by the oddness of having a blind man in the house, gets everyone some whiskey. The narrator is shocked that Robert doesn't wear sunglasses. He fixates on the sporadic movement and altered appearance of his eyes. As they talk about the flight across country and the train ride up from New York, the narrator is taken off guard again by the fact that Robert smokes, having heard that the blind didn't smoke because they couldn't see what they exhaled. His preconceptions are beginning to shatter.

Before long, dinner is served. They eat steak, devouring everything in front of them and talking little. The narrator is impressed by the skill with which Robert uses his utensils. He seems to know where everything exists on his plate. After dinner, they all adjourn to the living room, where the narrator's wife and Robert talk about old times. When the dialogue dulls a bit, the narrator turns on the television and his wife gets upset, thinking that her guest would not appreciate television. But consistent with his character, Robert defies expectations and admits that he has two televisions, claiming also that he prefers the color TV to his black and white one. Eventually, the narrator's wife decides to change into her robe, leaving her husband and Robert alone with the television.

The narrator offers Robert another drink and the two of them sit through the weather and sports report. The narrator's wife takes longer than expected to return, so the narrator asks Robert if he'd like to smoke a joint. Robert agrees, and soon after they start smoking, the narrator's wife comes downstairs. She is surprised to see Robert sharing a joint with her husband, but Robert just says there's a first time for everything. The narrator's wife also takes a few drags from the joint but falls asleep almost immediately afterward.

The narrator asks Robert if he'd like to go to bed, but Robert says he'd prefer to stay up, if it was all right. The narrator says he'd appreciate the company, realizing only after he says it that he genuinely would. When the news program ends, the narrator changes the channel. Unable to find anything good, he leaves the station on a program about churches and the Middle Ages. Eventually the program turns its focus to European cathedrals. During a long vocal pause, where the camera just roves around the various cathedral's, the narrator feels compelled to speak. He explains what is being shown and asks if Robert knows what a cathedral looks like. Robert admits that he knows little more than what was said on television and asks if the narrator could describe one to him.

The narrator stares hard at the screen and tries to figure out how he would go about it. He mentions that they are big and often made of stone or marble, but he can say little more than that. Finally he concedes that he can't really explain the appearance of a cathedral. He apologizes. Though Robert understands, he asks him if he'd be willing to draw one on some heavy paper. The narrator finds a paper bag from the kitchen and brings it into the living room. Robert tells him to sit on the floor beside him and allow his hand to ride on the narrator's as he draws the cathedral. Though the narrator is no artist, he does his best to capture the highlights of a cathedral. When he pauses, Robert runs his hands over the lines and encourages him to keep going. Eventually the narrator's wife wakes up and asks what they're doing. Robert tells her that they are drawing a cathedral together.

Robert suggests that they put people inside the cathedral, asking the narrator to close his eyes and draw them blind. So with Robert's hand still riding his, they continue to draw. "It was like nothing else in my life," the narrator admits. Even after Robert asks him to check it out, he doesn't want to open his eyes. "'It's really something,'" he says finally, still keeping his eyes closed.

LIST OF CHARACTERS IN

"Cathedral"

The Narrator, never named, is uncomfortable about the fact that a blind friend of his wife's is spending the night at their house. As the evening progresses, they eat and drink and the narrator gradually grows more comfortable. After several drinks, the narrator and his wife share a joint with Robert, the blind man. The narrator's wife falls asleep almost immediately, but Robert and the narrator stay up, watching and listening to television. Eventually, a show on cathedrals comes on and the narrator asks Robert if he knows what a cathedral looks like. The story ends with the narrator drawing a picture of a cathedral while Robert's hands are clasped on top.

The Narrator's Wife has invited her blind friend Robert, whom she hasn't seen in ten years, over for the night. They have traded tapes regularly since she worked for him back in Seattle. She cooks dinner for her husband and Robert, and shares drinks and a joint with them. After falling asleep on the couch, she wakes up to find her husband and Robert drawing a cathedral on a paper bag.

Robert is the blind friend of the narrator's wife. He flew east from Seattle to visit with the parents of his deceased wife, and asked to spend the night at the narrator's wife's house. He eats and drinks and smokes and talks with the narrator and his wife. The story ends with the narrator drawing a picture of a cathedral while Robert's hands are clasped on top.

"Cathedral"

IRVING HOWE ON STORIES OF OUR LONELINESS

[Irving Howe is the author and editor of many books and
critical studies including *World of Our Fathers, William
Faulkner: A Critical Study,* and *Politics of the Novel.* In this
excerpt, Howe speaks on the development of Carver's fiction, seen throughout the stories in *Cathedral.*]

In Cathedral a few stories move past Mr. Carver's expert tautness
and venture on a less secure but finer rendering of experience. The
title story is a lovely piece about a blind man who asks an acquaintance to guide his hand in sketching a cathedral he has never seen.
At the end, the two hands moving together, one guided by sight and
the other not, come to seem a gesture of fraternity.

The most interesting example of the changes in Mr. Carver's
work can be seen by comparing two versions of the same story. The
Bath, which appeared in an earlier collection, and A Small, Good
Thing, which appears in Cathedral. It is a story about a pleasant
young couple whose boy is soon to have a birthday. The parents
order a cake from a somewhat sullen baker, but before the birthday
can be celebrated the boy is hurt in an accident and the parents must
watch helplessly as he dies. Meanwhile the baker, as if he were some
evil spirit of harassment, keeps phoning the parents to pick up the
cake. In the first version, the story ends here abruptly, with the baker
calling still again.

The second version, nearly three times as long, goes beyond the
ending of the first. Now the parents visit the baker, berating him for
his phone calls and telling him the birthday boy has died. The baker
answers: Let me say how sorry I am. . . . Forgive me if you can. I'm
not an evil man, I don't think. Not evil, like you said. . . . I don't
know how to act anymore. (. . .)

Now, I'm pretty sure most teachers of creative writing would tell
their students that the first version is the better one. It's tighter and
more cryptic, and it gives critics a chance to carry on about symbolism.

But the teachers would be wrong. The second version, though less tidy and glittering, reaches more deeply into a human situation and transforms the baker from an abstract evil force into a flawed human creature. The first version, I would say, is a bit like second-rank Hemingway, and the second a bit like Sherwood Anderson at his best, especially in the speech rhythms of the baker.

Cathedral shows a gifted writer struggling for a larger scope of reference, a finer touch of nuance. What he has already done makes one eager to read his future work.

—Irving Howe, "Stories of Our Loneliness," *The New York Times Book Review*, (September 11, 1983): pp. 1, 42–3.

MARK A. R. FACKNITZ ON THE TRANSCENDENCE OF THE CHARACTERS

[Mark A. R. Facknitz is an essayist and a literary scholar whose work has appeared in such journals as *CEA Critic* and *Studies in Short Fiction*. In this excerpt, Facknitz discusses the rare transcendence that takes place with the characters in "Cathedral."]

Carver's characters rarely achieve a transcendent acceptance of their condition as does Ann Weiss. Indeed, more commonly they resign themselves without struggle or thought. They are rarely attractive people, and often readers must work against a narrator's tendency to sound cretinous or Carver's propensity to reveal characters as bigots and dunces. As the story opens, the first-person narrator of "Cathedral" appears to be another in this series of unattractive types. He worries about the approaching visit of a friend of his wife, a blind man named Robert who was once the wife's employer. He has little experience with the blind and faces the visit anxiously. His summary of the wife's association with Robert is derisive, its syntax blunt and its humor fatiguing:

> She'd worked with this blind man all summer. She read stuff to him, case studies, reports, that sort of thing. She helped him organize his little office in the county social service department.

They'd become good friends my wife and the blind man. How do I know these things? She told me. And she told me something else. On her last day in the office, the blind man asked if he could touch her face. She agreed to this. She told me he ran his fingers over every part of her face, her nose—even her neck! She never forgot it. She even tried to write a poem about it. She was always writing a poem. She wrote a poem or two every year, usually after something really important happened to her. (210)

Clearly he is jealous, and so emphasizes the eroticism of the blind man's touch. But she was leaving the blind man's office to marry her childhood sweetheart, an officer in the Air Force whom the narrator refers to as "this man who'd first enjoyed her favors" (210), and much of his jealousy toward the first husband transfers to the blind man Robert. Thus Robert sexually threatens the narrator, with his blindness, and by virtue of being a representative of a past that is meaningful to the wife. The narrator is selfish and callous; however, he is one of Carver's heavy drinkers and no reader could be drawn through "Cathedral" because he cares for him, and perhaps what pushes one into the story is a fear of the harm he may do to his wife and her blind friend. Yet Carver redeems the narrator by releasing him from the figurative blindness that results in a lack of insight into his own condition and which leads him to trivialize human feelings and needs. Indeed, so complete is his misperception that the blind man gives him a faculty of sight that he is not even aware that he lacks.

—Mark A. R. Facknitz, "'The Calm,' 'A Small Good Thing,' and 'Cathedral': Raymond Carver and the Discovery of Human Worth," *Studies in Short Fiction*, Vol. 23, No. 3 (Summer, 1986): pp. 287–296.

ARTHUR A. BROWN ON RAYMOND CARVER AND POSTMODERN HUMANISM

[Arthur A. Brown is an essayist and a scholar who has done literary study at University of California, Davis, and published criticism in journals such as *Critique*. In this excerpt, Brown speaks on the movement from the existentialism of

Carver's earlier fiction, to the humanism found in stories like "Cathedral."]

When Raymond Carver wrote "Cathedral," he recognized that it was "totally different in conception and execution from any stories that [had] come before." He goes on to say, "There was an opening up when I wrote the story. I knew I'd gone as far the other way as I could or wanted to go, cutting everything down to the marrow, not just to the bone. Any farther in that direction and I'd be at a dead end" (Fires, 204). He began to write longer stories, and his characters started to see things more clearly. Perhaps Carver was exaggerating, however, when he said that "Cathedral" was "totally" different.

Carver's writing has remained postmodern, a distinction as apparent as it is challenging to describe. The teacher of a drawing class once said as my class worked on contour drawings of a tree, "Don't lift your pencil from the page. Keep your eyes on the tree. Concentrate until you get a headache, until your pencil is on the branch of the tree." The contour drawing seems an apt metaphor for postmodern fiction, with its attention to surface detail, its resistance to depth, and its aspect of self-consciousness, where the medium merges with the subject—the creation of the fiction is the subject of the fiction. The pencil is on the tree. What can happen in postmodern fiction is what happened in that drawing class—when we looked down at the page, finally, we saw a good deal of contour drawing and little tree. What makes Carver's postmodern fiction so remarkable is that the tree is still there. He never loses sight of his subject, which is real life, even while his subject is also the creation of fiction.

"Cathedral" is the final story in the collection of stories by the same name; it is the first Carver wrote in this collection. William Stull characterizes the change the story represents in Carver's writing as a movement away from the "existential realism" of his earlier stories toward a "humanist realism."

> Existential realism . . . treats reality phenomenologically, agnostically, and objectively. Whether dead or in occultation, God—the archetype of the author—is absent from the world, which is discontinuous, banal, and, by definition, mundane. . . . The style of existential realism is, therefore, studiously objective, impersonal, and neutral. . . . Humanist realism, in contrast, takes

a more expressive, more "painterly" approach to its subjects. . . .
Such realism treats reality metaphysically, theologically, and sub-
jectively.

—Arthur A. Brown, "Raymond Carver and Postmodern Humanism,"
Critique, Vol 31, No. 2 (Winter, 1990): pp. 125-136.

TESS GALLAGHER ON THE WRITING OF "CATHEDRAL"

[Tess Gallagher, the widow of Raymond Carver, is a poet,
essayist, screenplay writer, and short story writer. Her published works include *Moon Crossing Bridge, A Concert of
Tenses* and *The Lover of Horses.* In this excerpt, Gallagher
describes the process that went into writing the breakthrough story "Cathedral."]

One story which was rather a breakthrough for Ray after *What We
Talk About When We Talk About Love* was "Cathedral," which he
began writing in the fall of 1982 on the train to New York City from
Syracuse. My friend Jerry Carriveau had phoned from Maryland to
say he wanted to visit us. His wife had recently died of cancer, and
he'd come east to spend time with her relatives. Jerry had been blind
since birth and in 1970 I'd taken a job working with him for the
Seattle Police Department for a year. Our job in the Research and
Development Department involved, among other tasks, devising a
single-print retrieval file system for fingerprints. In preparation for
Jerry's visit, I'd told Ray how I'd drawn fingerprint patterns out on
a tablet for my friend in such a way that they formed a raised surface. Then I'd guided his hand over them, simultaneously giving him
a verbal description which corresponded to what he was feeling
under his fingertips. Ray was masterful in converting this detail
when he fictionalized the visit of a blind man in "Cathedral." He
caused the blind man's hand to rest on top of the narrator's, thereby
placing the narrator in the position of making the recognitions—not
the other way around as it had been in the actual instance—and also
increasing the intimacy between the characters.

Ray generally hand-drafted his stories in one or two sittings. He secluded himself in his room and appeared only for cups of coffee or to check the mail. But "Cathedral" was drafted on a train paralleling the Hudson River, the very train that Jerry had taken from New York City for our reunion. Ray and I had been given the loan of an apartment for our stay in the city by a friend who was to be away for a few days. This trip was to have been a vacation, a time to see films and plays, and to eat at some good restaurants. It was the first free time we'd had in a long while. But instead of going out on the town, we both fell with a vengeance to our work and didn't venture out except in the evenings.

—Tess Gallagher, "Carver Country," *Carver Country* (New York: Charles Scribner's Sons, 1990): pp. 8-19.

TOM JENKS ON CARVER, GALLAGHER, AND "CATHEDRAL"

[Tom Jenks is the former senior editor at Scribner's. He is the author of *Our Happiness*, a novel, and he co-edited, along with Raymond Carver, the anthology *American Short Story Masterpieces*. In this excerpt, Jenks speaks of the germ for the story "Cathedral," and how both Carver and Tess Gallagher each wrote a fictional version of the events.]

I first met Ray Carver in New York in early September 1984 at a publishing dinner to launch Gary Fisketjon's Vintage Contemporary paperback series. Many of the new VC authors and their friends were there: Richard Ford, Toby Wolff, Jay McInerney, Tom McGuane, Jim Crumley, and Ralph Beer—a distinctly male crowd, and what struck me most was that, as we geared up to move to a nightclub, Ray, amid teasing about running off somewhere to see a woman, put himself in a taxi and headed for his hotel room alone. By the ginger way he got himself into the cab and laughingly ducked the barbs all around him, there was no doubt he meant to keep himself out of trouble.

But he was fair game for the friendly taunts that followed him into the cab. We were witnessing the Good Ray, but we all knew about the Bad Ray, the one who used to be Lord Misrule himself.

Reformed, Ray was fast becoming the most famous short story writer in the world, and the facts of his life were well known, partly because they were often the stuff of his writing and because fame brings a peculiar public intimacy.

At the time, I was an editor of *Esquire* and had made Ray's acquaintance through the mail and on the phone. I had published some of his work and knew him somewhat, and as I watched him slip away in the cab, I imagined him going back to his hotel room (it was early yet—ten o'clock) and telephoning Tess Gallagher at their home in Syracuse. Each evening they set aside the hours beyond ten o'clock to spend with each other. He *was*, in a sense, running off to see a woman.

A year and a half later, I visited them in Syracuse. During the days, Ray and I read stories for a book we were working on and at night we watched TV. One night, we were watching a PBS version of *Wuthering Heights*, and Ray began tell about another night of TV: the night the blind man for whom Tess once worked had come to visit. Tess told her side, too—how Ray was uneasy about the man's visit, uncomfortable with his blindness and his familiarity with Tess, a mild jealousy rising in Ray. Their evening was slow and tedious, and ended with the three of them watching PBS, just as we were. But on the night the blind man was visiting, Tess had fallen asleep, and then a program about cathedrals came on. The blind man had no idea what a cathedral looked like, and, in the end, Ray sat on the floor with him, holding his hands, drawing a cathedral so the blind man could sense the miracle of the shape.

Ray had written this story and titled it "Cathedral." Tess, who with Ray's encouragement had recently begun writing stories, had her own version, titled "The Harvest." She gave me a copy, humorously telling Ray, "Watch out, I'm nipping at your heels." Their good-natured competition and openness was rare in my experience of writers, many of whom are cagey about the intimate, personal connections in their work.

—Tom Jenks, "Shameless," *Remembering Ray: A Composite Biography of Raymond Carver*, eds. William L. Stull and Maureen P. Carroll. (Capra Press, 1993): pp. 141-143.

[Melvin Jules Bukiet is a professor of Fiction Writing at Sarah Lawrence College. He is the author of several novels and short story collections including *Signs and Wonders* and *While the Messiah Tarries.* In this excerpt, Bukiet speaks on the lack of specificity and empathy in Carver's earlier, widely influential fiction, and how he was just beginning to paint a more realized picture with stories such as "Cathedral."]

Carver aims to create a literature of reality, and so far as there are fiat gray lives of blunt actuality on any street corner, he does succeed in portraying them. Literature abounds in depictions of sordid or mediocre people, but it usually avoids the simply void. If the unexamined life is not worth living, then perhaps the unlived life is not worth examining.

Similarly, the dull, plodding march of subjects and predicates in the prose reflects a willful immersion in banality. "It was already dark. It was early in November and the days were short and cool." The passive construction echoes the passivity of his characters' lives and denies their individuality in favor of a numb; universal nihilism.

Carver's own teacher, John Gardner, whom the self-defined acolyte recalls lovingly in the essay collection Fires (Vintage, 204), wrote with a tenacious moral fervor and high ambition, Yet Gardner's definition of fiction as a "vivid and continuous dream" is the antithesis of his student's. For the most part, Carver's world is deliberately unvivid, undreamlike, and discontinuous in the extreme, so that the few episodes it entails could be reshuffled without damage. Most of his stories don't really develop; they simply terminate. "One More Thing" comes to a screeching halt when L.D., a drunk about to leave his wife and daughter, announces:" 'I just want to say one more thing.' But then he could not think what it could possibly be."

Ultimately, here's where Carver's influence lies, because the students who adore him have been absolved by him of the artist's responsibility to think through the consequences of characters' actions and perceptions. They can read him and say, "I can do that."

And the amazing thing is that they're right. By removing themselves from the humanity of their characters and simultaneously expunging their language of any element of either play or rigor, they become as meager as the lives they present. This has led inexorably to the smug, minor-key, often first-person narratives of so many first novels that can be summed up as "me and my problem."

In fact, Carver may have intuited these limitations himself, because the last stories he wrote start shifting toward greater specificity as well as empathy. "Cathedral" introduces us to a blind man who asks Carver's typically boorish protagonist to help him draw something remarkable, and "A Small, Good Thing" concludes with a moment of communion over a birthday cake baked for a dead child. Both present startlingly quirky images and coherent narratives. Perhaps if Carver hadn't died in 1988 his next collection would have moved fully into particularity and maybe it wouldn't have satisfied his core audience so deeply.

—Melvin Jules Bukiet, "Raymond Carver's Little America," *Village Voice*, (7/14/98, Vol. 43, Issue 28): p. 129.

"Fever"

"Fever," a third person narrative from Carver's collection *Cathedral*, opens as the main character, Carlyle, worries about finding a suitable baby sitter for his children, Sarah and Keith, now that the summer's over and he has to go back to his high school teaching job. Carlyle's wife, Eileen, left him and his children at the beginning of the summer to pursue her own art.

The narrative goes into back story at this point and explains that Eileen had left with one of Carlyle's colleagues, Richard Hoopes, to Southern California. Richard taught drama and glass blowing at the high school where Carlyle teaches art. Eileen and Richard left just after the end of the semester.

The first sitter that Carlyle finds is a teenage girl named Debbie. He is so desperate to find someone that he places his children in Debbie's hands "as if she were a relative." He is surprised and upset at himself when he comes home early one day to find his children out side alone with a big dog and another person's car in the driveway. When he walks inside, he finds three teenage boys in the living room, drinking beer and smoking cigarettes, while Debbie is on the couch with another boy. Everyone jumps to their feet when Carlyle walks in. Debbie pleads, above a blaring Rod Stewart record, for the opportunity to explain, but Carlyle tells her and the rest of the crew to get out of his house. Before she leaves, Debbie reminds him that he owes her money, but says that he doesn't have to pay her for today. After everyone leaves, Carlyle promises his children pizza for dinner.

Later that night, after Sarah and Keith go to sleep, Carlyle calls Carol, a secretary in the principal's office from his school, with whom he's begun to spend time. Carol offers to find a sitter for her son Dodge, so she could keep Carlyle company, but he declines and thanks her for her thoughtfulness.

The narrative shifts again to back story, describing how Carlyle had spent nearly every minute with his children after Eileen left, reading to them and assuring them that their mother would eventually return. But when they went to sleep, his feelings would swing dramatically, one minute yearning for Eileen to come home, and the next, wishing her nothing but ill will. It was during this time when he contacted an employment agency and asked for someone to baby sit and keep house. The agency sent over a cold, hairy woman who barely acknowledged Sarah and Keith—Carlyle opted not to hire her. It was then that he came upon a sign in the super market advertising baby sitting services. This is how he first hired Debbie.

Throughout the course of the summer, Eileen sends cards and letters and photographs of herself to Sarah and Keith, along with some of her own pen-and-ink drawings. She also sends letters to Carlyle claiming that she's happy and hoping that he could understand, insisting that a love bond still existed between them. Though Carlyle initially crumples up the letter, he eventually takes it out of the trash and places it with a picture she sent of herself.

The narrative continues back further still, and tells of when they first fell in love. Even then, Eileen had said that she planned to do something with her artistic talent. At the time, Carlyle was in full support. Eight years after they were married, she acted by moving to Southern California with Richard Hoopes.

Although Carlyle is tempted to call Eileen and tell her about the babysitting situation, he decides against it. He has only called her once since she left and it had been humiliating for him. Richard Hoopes answered the phone and spoke to him as if they were buddies. Then he handed the phone to Eileen who inquired about Carlyle's well being, speaking of his karma and claiming that it was going to improve. Carlyle wondered whether she was losing her mind. As he thinks about the awkwardness of this conversation, the phone rings, and he knows even before answering that it's Eileen.

Carlyle admits that he's been thinking about her, regretting his admission moments after it comes out of his mouth. Eileen claims to have sensed that something was wrong and says she knows that he's in need of a baby sitter. She tells him of a woman named Mrs. Webster who used to work for Richard's mother. She is supposed to be wonderful, she tells her husband, mentioning that Richard had already spoken with her earlier that evening, and she is supposed to call Carlyle that night or the following morning. Then she asks Carlyle to send her love to Sarah and Keith and tell them that their mother will be sending more pictures. She says she doesn't want them to forget that she's an artist.

An hour later, the phone rings and an older woman introduces herself as Mrs. Jim Webster. Carlyle asks if she can show up early the next morning and she agrees, assuring him that she can be counted on. At seven the next morning, after Carlyle has showered and gotten dressed for the day, a pick-up truck pulls in the driveway and Mrs. Webster gets out. Carlyle invites her into the house, and wakes up Sarah and Keith so they can meet her. When it's clear that she will be staying on for the day, Mrs. Webster asks Carlyle to wave at her husband who is outside in their truck, so he knows that she'll be staying. With a good feeling about Mrs. Webster, Carlyle gathers his stuff and heads out to work. "For the first time in months, it seemed, he felt his burden had lifted a little."

Carlyle's contentment carries over into his teaching, as he is relaxed and confident and more long-winded than usual. At lunch, he acts affectionately toward Carol, despite the fact that their relationship is not public knowledge. Carlyle tells her about Mrs. Webster and how good her arrival has made him feel. Then he clutches her knee beneath the table and asks her to come to his house later that night.

When he arrives home from work, his children are bathed and clothed and in the kitchen helping Mrs. Webster bake cookies. Mrs. Webster tells Carlyle that Eileen called to say "'what goes around, comes around.'" A few hours later, Carlyle reads to his children and puts them to bed. Then he gets a drink and waits for Carol. Eventually she arrives and before long they end up in bed. When the phone rings, Carlyle refuses to answer it, claiming that it's his wife and that she's lost her mind. Carol eventually goes, having clearly enjoyed herself with Carlyle.

The narrative resumes six weeks later. Mrs. Webster has made an enormous difference in Carlyle's life. He is more at peace now and able to think about Eileen without the same degree of hatred and distress. He is spending more time with Carol, until he falls ill. On the first day of his fever, he calls school and tells them to get Mel Fisher to substitute—a committed artist who refuses to show his work. Mrs. Webster takes care of the children and does her best to look after Carlyle. After a while, when Carlyle is finally able to make it out of bed, he asks if Mr. Webster had been in the house earlier that day. Mrs. Webster says that he had, as he was hoping to meet Carlyle and tell him about their impending plans.

Just as Carlyle inquires as to the news, the phone rings. It's Eileen, claiming to have sensed Carlyle's illness. She says that Richard has also been sick and that there's something going around. Then she surprises him by asking whether he's still keeping a journal. He had told her several years earlier that he was keeping a journal, but had never shown it to her. Eileen suggests that he keep a record of his thoughts while he's ill, claiming that it can be an insightful period. She goes on to say that the French writer Colette had often done that. She says that Richard turned her on to Colette's work. Carlyle is convinced that she's losing her mind.

When he hangs up the phone, Mrs. Webster asks to talk to him. She tells him that her son, who lives in Oregon, has invited her and her husband to live with them and work on their mink farm. She says they are taking him up on the offer as they're getting old and it would mean not having to worry about what will happen once they get too old to take care of themselves. Mrs. Webster says that she'll finish out the week, but then she'll have to go.

Carlyle, still stricken with fever, starts to talk to Mrs. Webster about Eileen. He mentions that she had suggested writing his thoughts down. Then he talks about their feelings for one another when they first met, and how the most difficult thing for him right now is coming to terms with the fact that whatever happens in their lives from this point on, will not be shared by one another.

Carlyle continues to talk as Sarah and Keith come into the room and sit beside Mrs. Webster. Then Mr. Webster knocks on the door and his wife tells him to come in and sit down. Carlyle, without shame, continues to talk about his past with Eileen. Finally he has said all that he has to say and stops. Mrs. Webster assures him that both he and Eileen are good people and that things will turn out well for them. Then the Websters get up to leave and Carlyle shakes each of their hands. The story closes as Carlyle watches the Websters leave from his living room window, feeling that somehow things have been resolved, that he could accept the ending of the previous chapter of his life, and finally move on to the next. After waving to the Websters, he brings his arm down and turns to his children.

"Fever"

Carlyle is the first character the reader encounters. He is a high school art teacher whose wife, Eileen, left him earlier in the summer. Now that the school year is about to start up again, he needs to find a sitter for his children, Sarah and Keith. Carlyle had to fire the first sitter he hired, a high school girl name Debbie, after he caught her drinking and smoking in his house with other teenage boys. Eventually, his wife's boyfriend, one of Carlyle's former colleagues, contacts a woman named Mrs. Webster who had worked for his mother in the past. Mrs. Webster calls Carlyle and they arrange for her to watch the kids and clean the house. Mrs. Webster does a magnificent job and helps turn Carlyle's life around. But then he gets hit with a high fever which coincides with Mrs. Webster's announcement that she and her husband will be moving to Oregon. The story ends on a positive note, as Carlyle, still stricken by fever, feels as if he's entered a new phase in his life.

Mrs. Webster is the baby sitter/house keeper whom Carlyle hires to watch his children, Sarah and Keith. Mrs. Webster does an incredible job for Carlyle and helps him move on with his life. But then she and her husband accept an invitation to move in with their son in Oregon and she has to tell Carlyle that she's leaving.

Carol is a secretary in the principal's office at the school where Carlyle teaches. She and Carlyle get involved soon after Eileen leaves. Once Mrs. Webster starts working for Carlyle, Carol and Carlyle grow closer.

Eileen is Carlyle's wife. She is an artist who decides to move to Southern California with one of Carlyle's former colleagues, Richard Hoopes, to pursue her art. She calls Carlyle periodically after her departure, and often seems to know how he's feeling.

Richard Hoopes is one of Carlyle's former colleagues. He moves to Southern California with Eileen. He recommended Mrs. Webster to Carlyle.

Sarah and **Keith** are the children of Carlyle and Eileen.

Debbie is the first baby sitter whom Carlyle hires. She gets fired after Carlyle catches her drinking and smoking inside his house with other teenage boys.

"Fever"

MICHAEL J. BUGEJA ON HOPE IN THE STORY

[Michael J. Bugeja is an essayist and scholar whose criticism has appeared in such journals as *The South Dakota Review*. In this excerpt, Bugeja speaks about "Fever" as an example of one of the more hopeful stories that appears throughout the collection *Cathedral*.]

A similar ending occurs in Fever, a third-person story whose chief character, Carlyle, is learning to cope with the breakup of his marriage, while being father and mother to two children. Carlyle has another concernfinding a competent babysitterthe type of problem that can mushroom to colossal proportions in a Carver story. This one seems destined to do so. But the estranged wife, an aspiring artist who has run off with another school teacher and mutual friend, solves the problem long-distance via telephone. She puts her husband on to Mrs. Webster, a motherly figure who temporarily frees Carlyle from his troubles, as the narrative persona tells us in this passage:

> He believed his life was beginning again. Though he hadn't heard from Eileen since that call six weeks ago, he found himself able to think about her without being angry or else close to tears.

At this point we sense that circumstances are too right for a Carver story and that something will occur to destroy the serenity that depends on Mrs. Webster. Two things happen: Carlyle comes down with fever on the very day his babysitter tells him that she will be leaving with her husband for Oregon. She explains that her stepson has invited her and her husband to help with a mink ranch, a proposition they cannot refuse. She says of her husband: Jim won't have to worry anymore about what's going to happen to us. . . . He was sixty-two last week. He hasn't had anything for some time. The love the Websters share evokes a sympathetic response from Carlyle, who once thought he would grow old with his wife and now realizes that will never occur. The realization bonds Carlyle to the old woman, and he tells her about his love for Eileen and how the love went wrong. It is an ending skillfully handled through dialogue and commentary and one that never leaves Carlyle's point of view. Finally, the Websters must leave and Carlyle feels something end in his life. The last paragraph hints at the same kind of hope found in Where I'm Calling From:

> As the pickup lurched forward, he lifted his arm once more. He saw the old couple lean toward him briefly as they drove away. Then he brought his arm down and turned to his children.

The story, one of the best in the collection, also contains humor associated with Carlyle's wife. She has adopted a new lifestyle in California and writes rambling letters that proclaim That which is truly bonded can never become unbonded. She studies Carlyle's karma and advises him in telephone calls. She leaves absurd messages for himwhat goes around, comes aroundwith Mrs. Webster. But despite the wife's weirdness, she is often on target, from knowing that Carlyle needs a good sitter to sensing his sickness: "I know, don't ask me how, that things are not going so well right now.

> You're sick, aren't you?" Such humor serves a purpose. It creates an atmosphere similar to tragicomedy, a feeling that although things will worsen in the fiction, the characters will emerge better for it.

> —Michael J. Bugeja, "Tarnish and Silver: An Analysis of Carver's 'Cathedral,'" *The South Dakota Review*, (Vol. 24, No. 3, Autumn, 1986): pp. 73-87.

ARTHUR SALTZMAN ON CARLYLE'S MENTAL DEVELOPMENT

> [Arthur Saltzman is an essayist, biographer and literary scholar. His published works include *Understanding Raymond Carver.* In this excerpt, Saltzman discusses the role of mental health in the story.]

In like fashion the protagonist of "Fever" finds his anxieties mitigated by the basic inducements of human contact. One of the practical crises Carlyle must face in trying to deal with his abandonment by his wife, Eileen, for his colleague—a mutual friend and fellow high school art teacher "who'd apparently turned his grades in on time" (158)—is locating a dependable babysitter now that fall classes have begun again. His hurried choices, which include a careless teenager and a gruff, ghoulish woman with hairy arms, are disappointing and encourage his fear that Eileen's leaving has left unpluggable cracks everywhere.

Eileen telephones to solicit his understanding in "this matter" (recalling the plastic connotations of Inez's marital "assessment" in "Careful") and to verify her happiness, as though it might be of some indefinable consolation to him. Her unctuous earnestness exasperates him, especially because it is conveyed by the jargon of pop psychology: they are still "bonded," she is "going for it," they need to keep the "lines of communication open," he needs to adopt a "positive mental attitude," . . . and say, how's your karma? But despite what Carlyle deems her "insanity," Eileen is prescient enough to have realized that he needs a sitter for the children and a housekeeper. She provides the name of Mrs. Webster, an older woman who had once worked for Eileen's lover's mother (how civil! how sophisticated they are!) and whom she promises he can count on (in contrast, presumably, to her own inconstancy).

Whatever his doubts toward Eileen, Carlyle discovers in Mrs. Webster the kind of quiet dignity and supportiveness, particularly in her intimacies with her husband, that Holly had dreamed of in "Gazebo" as being the special province of the elderly, and indeed, that Carlyle had hoped would represent his future with Eileen. As a result of Mrs. Webster's taking over the household, Carlyle is suffused with calm; he becomes more intrepid in his relationship with his girlfriend (whom he had previously admired for her ability to equate understanding him with not pressuring him), and the family begins to thrive to the extent that Carlyle can face the truth about his wife's permanent decision not to return. When he falls ill, Mrs. Webster easily expands her ministrations to incorporate him as well as his children, and not even fever can deter his prospects for renewal, which have been due in large measure to Mrs. Webster's indiscriminate love.

When Mrs. Webster arrives one day with the news that she and her husband are leaving for Oregon to work on a mink ranch,

Carlyle's initial response is panic; to be sure, the sudden shattering of one's delicate composure is common enough throughout Carver's stories, and it would not be surprising for "Fever" to conclude with Carlyle dangling over the pit of his own disarray. Eileen calls again. She has intuited her husband's distress, for which she prescribes journal writing in order to translate and extinguish his problems. But once again Carlyle figures that her craziness contaminates the communication she extols.

Nevertheless, Carlyle is spared a final breakdown. He relates the history of his relationship with Eileen to the eternally patient Mrs. Webster, who bestows her acceptance and predicts his restoration: "'Good. Good for you,' Mrs. Webster said when she saw he had finished. 'You're made out of good stuff. And so is she—so is Mrs. Carlyle. And don't you forget it. You're both going to be okay after this is over'" (185). Consequently, Carlyle learns that he is ready to come to terms with life in the wake of loss. In fact, "loss" is a misnomer for the abiding legacy of his past, in that it "would become a part of him now, too, as surely as anything else he'd left behind" (186). Subdued, yet resolute, Carlyle turns away from the departing Websters and toward his children. This closing gesture implies his emergence from fever and vulnerability, if only to the degree that he is able to offer himself, which is the surest sign of health Carver ever provides.

—Arthur Saltzman, "Cathedral," Understanding Raymond Carver, (University of South Carolina press, 1988): pp. 124-156.

RANDOLPH PAUL RUNYON ON CARLYLE'S ACCEPTANCE

> [Randolph Paul Runyon is an essayist and a scholar whose published works include the book *Reading Raymond Carver.* In this excerpt, Runyon speaks on the mental effort put forth by the characters in the story.]

Arthur Saltzman accurately observes that the narrator of "Where I'm Calling From" "is at first unwilling or unable to relate his own story. . . . Instead of confessing, the narrator persuades a fellow drunk, J.P., to tell his" (147). The woman in "The Train" makes the same observation about Miss Dent: "You don't say much. But I'll wager you could say a lot if someone got you started. Couldn't you? But you're a sly boots. You'd rather just sit with your prim little mouth while other people talk their heads off" (153). The wife in "Fever" likewise urges the husband she has left to talk it out: "Tell me about yourself," she said on the phone. "He told her the kids were fine. But before he could say anything else, she interrupted him to say, 'I know they're fine. What about you?'" (165).

"Fever" is the account of Carlyle's eventually successful effort to accept his wife's not coming back. He teaches art at a high school; Eileen ran away with the drama teacher, leaving Carlyle to cope with his two young children alone. After some bad experiences with babysitters, his luck changes dramatically when his wife puts him in touch with the grandmotherly Mrs. Webster. For six weeks things go beautifully, until Carlyle comes down with a severe bout of the flu. His fever and headaches keep him in bed for several days, while Mrs. Webster takes care of both him and the children.

During this time Eileen occasionally telephones to ask how he is and to say that her life has significantly improved since she left him, all in a trendy psychobabble about her "karma" and his that convinces Carlyle she is going crazy. "Eileen must be losing her mind to talk like that" (164). Her perceived insanity is mentioned at least a half-dozen times in the story. On one occasion even Eileen shows that she realizes how strange she must sound: "'You may think I'm crazy or something,' she said. 'But just remember.' Remember what? Carlyle wondered in alarm, thinking he must have missed something she'd said" (168). On another Carlyle tells his girlfriend Carol why he's not going to answer the phone. "It's my wife. I know it's her. She's losing her mind. She's going crazy. I'm not going to answer it" (175). When he falls ill, Eileen advises him to keep a journal of his illness, just like Colette.7"She wrote a little book about what it was like, about what she was thinking and feeling the whole time she had this fever. . . . Right now you've just got this discomfort. You've got to translate that into something usable" (181). Carlyle can make no sense of what seemed like pointless advice. "It was clear to him that she was insane."

—Randolph Paul Runyon, "Reading Cathedral," *Reading Raymond Carver*, (Syracuse University Press, 1992): pp. 137-85.

[Ewing Campbell has been a professor of English at Texas A&M University. He is the author of *The Rincon Triptych* and *Piranesi's Dream*. In this excerpt, Campbell describes the story as being steeped in domestic melodrama.]

Carver's next story, "Fever," is not written with characteristic detachment. It sinks into domestic melodrama and suffers from comparison with "Cathedral" or, for that matter, with other works possessing the same theme: creative illness as initiating premise. Grounded in ancient shamanistic practice, wherein the shaman induces an ecstatic trance during which he divines the hidden, the theme has served literary texts well in the past, most notably Thomas Mann's *Doctor Faustus*. In that ambitious novel, Adrian Leverkuhn's syphilis produces musical genius, but here, as the source of the protagonist's resigned acceptance of his circumstances, the creative illness falls short.

Carlyle is the protagonist. His wife has left him and their children. As a teacher off for the summer, he manages to handle the domestic responsibilities for that period, but with school starting up again, he hires a sitter for the children. When she neglects them and behaves in an unacceptable manner, he is forced to let her go.

That is his quandary when his wife calls from California to let him know she and the man she is with have been working on Carlyle's problem, presumably known to them by extrasensory perception, and have called a Mrs. Webster to come to his aid. An unlikely coincidence, it brings the crucial Mrs. Webster into the story. She takes over the duties. All seems resolved: "That afternoon he arrived home to find his house neat and orderly and his children in clean clothes. In the kitchen, Keith and Sarah stood on chairs, helping Mrs. Webster with gingerbread cookies. Sarah's hair was out of her face and held back with a barrette" *(Where*, 238*)*.

Chaos has been banished; order is restored and symbolized in the children's behavior and the little girl's combed hair. But there must be conflict to make a story. Six weeks pass and all is fine until Carlyle becomes ill. Although Carlyle's wife has not called during the intervening six weeks, she contacts him now, saying that she knows he is sick—another incredible coincidence. Referring to Colette's having kept an account during one of her illnesses, Eileen urges Carlyle to keep a journal of his illness, too.

Apparently, she has a vague idea about creative illnesses and imagines that he is experiencing one. In such ordeals, the sufferer experiences painful symptoms accompanied by a dominating preoccupation. The sickness ends in a state of exhilaration, from which the sufferer emerges with a sense of permanent change and the marked conviction that a great truth has been discovered.

That is exactly what Carver is aiming for, but the wife makes an unconvincing medium for introducing the event. Nevertheless, the transformation occurs. Coming out of his illness, Carlyle learns that Mrs. Webster and her husband are going to move on to help her husband's son by an earlier marriage. This knowledge appears to break the barrier, and he begins to talk, telling her about the early years of his relation with Eileen, their love, their hopes, now lost.

He talks until his lingering headache vanishes, but he does not stop then. He continues even after his children come in and fall asleep on the floor, even after Mr. Webster comes in and quietly takes a chair. He talks everything out of his system in a burst of cathartic confession. As she and her husband are leaving, Mrs. Webster says that she will see him the next morning:

> As if something important had been settled, Carlyle said, "Right!" The old couple went carefully along the walk and got into their truck. . . . It was then, as he stood at the window, that he felt something had come to an end. It had to do with Eileen and the life before this. . . . But he understood it was over, and he felt able to let her go. . . . [I]t was something that had passed. And that passing—though it had seemed impossible and he'd fought against it—would become a part of him now, too, as surely as anything else he'd left behind. (*Where*, 247)

—Ewing Campbell, "Maturity: Cathedral," *Raymond Carver: A Study of the Short Fiction*. (New York: Twayne Publishers, 1992): pp. 48-70.

"The Bridle"

"The Bridle" is a first person narrative told by a woman named Marge who manages an Arizona apartment building along with her husband Harley. The action opens as an old station wagon with Minnesota plates pulls into the parking lot. There is a couple in the front seat and two boys in the back, all of whom look worn out. They get out of their car and knock on Marge and Harley's door. Marge invites them in and asks if they are looking for an apartment. The man says they are looking for an apartment and introduces himself as Holits.

As the narrative continues, the reader is told that in addition to renting apartments, Marge is also a hair stylist. There is a professional size hair drier in the corner of the living room. She also has business cards and a stockpile of old magazines, for people to read while they're waiting for their hair to dry.

Marge shows Holits and his wife, Betty, a furnished apartment and tells them that she'll need first and last months rent as well as a security deposit if they want to take it. She asks Holits what he does for a living, and his wife answers that he's a farmer. They had a farm in Minnesota, Betty explains, adding that her husband also knows a lot about horses. Marge suspects that Holits is unemployed, and feels a bit sorry for him. After they agree to take the apartment, they all return to the office where Holits pays what they owe in cash. With the transaction complete, he turns to his wife and says "'Arizona. Never thought you'd see Arizona, did you?'"

The narrator watches Holits and his family unload their wagon, paying particular attention to an object, which she finally realizes is a bridle. As Holits and his family continue to unload their wagon, Marge thinks about the bills with which Holits had paid. She takes them out of the drawer and decides to write her name on one of them, imaging all the places the bill could end up, and fantasizing about someone finding it and wondering who she is. When Harley finally comes in from cutting the grass, he asks about the new family from Minnesota, referring to them as Swedes. Marge responds by saying that they're not Swedes, but Harley doesn't seem to listen.

The following afternoon, Marge watches the boys clean their wagon and swim in the pool. Because it's a weekend, there are others at the pool too. Irving Cobb, who everyone calls Spuds, is laying out with his wife Linda. Connie Nova, who had originally moved in with her fiancé but is now living with a long-haired college student named Rick, is also poolside. Spuds had lost his wife just before moving into the building, but three months later, he married Linda. Marge is reminded of an off evening that she and Harley spent with Spuds and Linda. They were at their apartment and Irving decided to show home videos of a trip to Alaska he took with his first wife, Evelyn. The strange part was that he didn't seem to want to shut the movie off, so eventually Marge and Harley left.

Marge is reminded of another party that she and Harley went to at Connie Nova's place when Connie was still engaged to the alcoholic lawyer. Marge and Harley barely talked to any one and didn't stay long. They finally left after Connie's fiancé had a drawing for a free divorce. He had everyone pick out of a hat and the woman who drew the voucher for free representation was elated at having won.

A week after the arrival of Holits' family, Betty finds a job as a waitress, but Holits, who spends his entire day inside, still seems unemployed. Marge found out most of what she knows about Holits and his family after Betty made an appointment to get her hair done. It was then that Betty told her that the children are from Holits' first wife who left him on New Years Day over ten years ago. She says she loves them as though if they were her own. Then she tells Marge how they got to be where they are now. She says that things were fine until Holits got involved with horses. He apparently bought a racehorse, who he named Fast Betty, and started racing her at the track. Though Betty didn't know it at the time, Holits was placing money on this horse to win every time it raced, only it lost every time. Marge gives her a manicure, saying the first one is on the house, and starts to tell Betty a bit about her own situation, when Harley walks into the room. Before long, Marge finishes her work with Betty. "'You look brand new, honey,'" Marge says. "'Don't I wish,'" Betty replies.

A few months later, Holits and Betty are drinking out by the pool with Irving and Linda Cobb, and Connie Nova and her boyfriend Rick. It's about ten at night and they're all pretty drunk. Marge watches them from her window, debating whether to enforce the building rule that no one can be poolside after ten. Harley, who would surely enforce the regulation, is asleep and Marge is buying time before she wakes him. As Marge watches them outside, Holits starts climbing up to the roof of the Cabana, convinced he can make the leap from the cabana to the pool. While he's up on the roof, everyone except for his wife, Betty, is cheering him on. He backs up, rubs his hands together, and gets a running start before he jumps from roof, landing on the deck instead of the pool. Marge runs outside and says they should take him to the hospital. His forehead is bleeding badly and he seems uncertain about everything around him. The group piles into one car, and despite being inebriated, drive Holits to the hospital.

Following that day, Marge doesn't see Betty going to work anymore and she almost never sees Holits leaving the house. When she does see him, he acts as if she's a stranger. Finally, one of Holits' and Betty's sons comes by with a note saying that they're leaving. Connie and Spuds are by the pool when Holits and his family are packing the car. They wave at him, but he doesn't seem to recognize them. Finally he raises his hand in response, but does little more.

After they leave, Marge stands between the TV and her husband, responding to some inner urge to communicate. But Harley just stares dumbfounded before the phone rings and they never get a chance to connect. Marge decides to ignore the phone and goes up to the apartment that the Holits' family just vacated. While looking around, she finds the bridle that she had seen them carry in on their first day there. She wonders whether it was left on purpose and reflects on the nature of a bridle, how it's fit over a horse's mouth to help direct it. "When you felt it pull, you'd know it was time. You'd know you were going somewhere."

LIST OF CHARACTERS IN

"The Bridle"

Marge is the narrator of the story and the first character the reader encounters. She and her husband Harley work for the corporation that owns their apartment building. Marge also works independently as a hair stylist. She takes particular interest in a family from Minnesota who move into one of the apartments in their building. The wife, Betty, hires Marge on one occasion to do her hair, and Betty tells her about how her husband's investment in a racehorse was the beginning of their downfall. This family leaves soon after the husband, Holits, gets into an accident on the deck of the swimming pool and injures his head. After they leave, Marge goes into their apartment to clean their place and finds a horse's bridle that was left behind.

Harley is Marge's husband. He is the manager of the apartment building in which they live. He refers to the family from Minnesota as The Swedes.

Betty is the wife of Holits and the stepmother of Holits' two sons. She reveals to Marge, while getting her hair done, that she is not the natural mother of the two boys. Soon after moving in, she gets a job as a waitress at an Italian restaurant.

Holits is a former farmer from Minnesota who is forced to sell his property after he invests all his money in a racehorse that never pays off. One drunken evening, Holits climbs on top of the cabana by the pool and tries to jump from the roof into the water. Unfortunately, he does not make it and lands hard on the deck, injuring his head. Following the incident, Holits seems to be perpetually confused. Before long, he and his family leave.

Irving and **Linda Cobb** are residents of the apartment building where the story takes place. They were married three months after Irving's first wife had passed away. They are drinking with Holits when he attempts to jump from the cabana roof into the pool.

Connie Nova and **Rick** are residents of the apartment building where the story takes place. Connie was previously engaged to a lawyer who raffled off a free divorce. They are drinking with Holits when he attempts to jump from the cabana roof into the pool.

"The Bridle"

JAMES W. GRINNEL REVIEWS THE COLLECTION *CATHEDRAL*

> [James W. Grinnel is an essayist and scholar whose criti-
> cism has appeared in such journals as *Studies in Short
> Fiction.* In this excerpt, Grinnel speaks about the new
> heights reached by Carver in stories such as "The Bridle."]

And now comes Cathedral a book with a one-word title and a dozen,
more fully fleshed-out stories. They are still hard little gems of fiction but they are a few carats heavier than those of the earlier books.
Six of the twelve are first person narrations; all are restricted to their
characters' stunted perspectives, which is to say, to Carver's tight
control. He does not mock his people nor does he suggest that their
lives would be improved if they examined them, if they were to
expect, inspect and introspect more. A kind of literary minimalist,
Carver simply presents his people and their stark lives as if there
were nothing richer out there, no American milieu of affluence, of
new horizons, of hope. We readers have to carry our own emotional
baggage to and from these stories because Carver will not porter for
us.

For example, in the opening story, "Feathers," the lethargic rou-
tine of the narrator and his wife is broken when a coworker invites
them home for dinner. And a strange home it is, furnished with a T.V.
upon which sits a plaster of Paris cast of crooked teeth, and before
the television a La-Z-Boy chair for the host. This host has an odd little wife, plump and retiring, to whom the crooked teeth once
belonged, and together they have a pet peacock and a fat ugly baby.
Says the narrator, "Bar none, it was the ugliest baby I'd ever seen. It
was so ugly I couldn't say anything. No words would come out of
my mouth."

This was not the only time words failed him. As the evening wore
on, it became very special for him despite the almost grotesque
assemblage. Because he could not quite articulate that special quality,

he closed his eyes to freeze a picture of it forever in his memory. It worked but ironically, because that evening was the beginning of an even drabber life for the narrator and his wife. They went home and conceived a child who later developed "a conniving streak in him." They never return the invitation and now "mostly it's just the TV."

So it goes with Carver's characters. Often they experience a special moment which almost affords them a glimpse of something elusive—a better life perhaps. But they cannot quite fathom the experience and so they retreat to drink or to dull routines made somehow even duller by the missed chance.

One of the stories, "The Compartment" is set entirely on a train in Europe and concerns a failed father-son reunion. Another, dedicated to one of Carver's former drinking partners, John Cheever, is entitled "The Train" and is set entirely in a suburban New York train station. In this story Carver seems to be paying tribute to Cheever by using Cheeveresque elements in a way not entirely unlike what John Updike did in the "Bech Wed" section of Bech Is Back.

But for the most part, Raymond Carver sticks with and refines familiar territory and people. Using these familiar elements, he reaches new heights in a story called "The Bridle" and peaks in the title story, "Cathedral." This little masterpiece concludes with its first person narrator trying to describe to a blind man a cathedral that he sees on television. When words fail, he tries to express the experience by holding the man's hand while sketching a cathedral. The blind man, really more perceptive than he, has the narrator close his eyes. He achieves a new dimension of perception. He tells us, "My eyes were still closed. I was in my house. I knew that. But I didn't feel like I was inside anything! 'It's really something,' I said."

—James W. Grinnel, "A Review of Cathedral,'" *Studies in Short Fiction*, (Vol. 21, No. 1, Winter, 1984): pp. 71–72.

[Patricia Schnapp has been a professor of English at Bowling Green State University. In this excerpt, Schnapp discusses the inarticulateness of Carver's characters.]

Frank Kermode has declared that Carver is a master of the short form, and Carver's "A Small, Good Thing," which is included in this collection, was this year's first place winner in William Abraham's distinguished annual "Prize Stories: The O. Henry Awards."

There is no melodrama in Carver's spare, laconic, but brilliantly evocative fiction. "Vitamins," for instance, begins: "I had a job and Patti didn't. I worked a few hours a night for the hospital." Patti does get herself a job, however, "for her self-respect." She sells vitamins door to door. Eventually the narrator attempts to have an affair with one of his wife's co-workers, but it is aborted by the advances of a black man at a "spade club" the couple goes to. The frustrated narrator returns home. His wife hears him and, thinking she has overslept, gets up and dresses. The story concludes:

> I couldn't take any more tonight. "Go back to sleep, honey. I'm looking for something," I said. I knocked some stuff out of the medicine chest. Things rolled into the sink. "Where's the aspirin?" I said. I knocked down some more things. I didn't care. Things kept falling.

Things do keep falling in Carver's fictional world. With just a few exceptions, he suggests throughout his stories that we are victims of the continuous collapse of our hopes. In "The Bridle," one of the characters says significantly, "Dreams, you know, are what you wake up from."

At times in his fiction adultery or alcoholism or estrangement afflicts a marital relationship, but always there is the problem of communication, for Carver's characters are essentially inarticulate. But it is precisely their inarticulateness that haunts us. It is what they do not say, what the author refuses to divulge, that is nuanced with menace, tinged with sinister suggestion. Under the quiet surfaces of his stories throb foreboding hints of disintegration and disaster. Carver's characters, of course, reflect our own inarticulateness, our inability to tell others of our anxieties and expectations, of the random and confused impulses which determine our behavior. He writes of our silences.

But these silences in Carver are like the ominous silence before a storm. They portend danger. And we read his stories with increasing alertness and mounting apprehension, waiting for and expecting the worst. Only rarely, as in the title story, do we see, and through a most unlikely agent—in this case, a blind man—the towering cathedral of our possibilities.

—Patricia Schnapp, "A Review of Cathedral," *Western American Literature*, (Vol. 20, No. 2, Summer, 1985): pp. 168-69.

EWING CAMPBELL ON THE SYMPATHY IN THE NARRATOR

[Ewing Campbell has been a professor of English at Texas A&M University. He is the author of *The Rincon Triptych* and *Piranesi's Dream*. In this excerpt, Campbell discusses the sympathy of the narrator in the story.]

Sympathy emanates from Carver's enterprising narrator-apartment manager, Marge, who has installed a professional chair with sink and turned the front room of her living quarters into a beauty parlor, where she collects the rents, writes receipts and, most important, talks to interested parties. As up-to-date as any current member of the National Hairdressers and Cosmetologists Association, she disdains the title of beautician and calls herself a stylist.

In charge of a corporate-owned apartment complex in Arizona, Marge and her husband, Harley, observe the arrival of a family of four in flight from the chaos of their life in Minnesota. Marge rents them an apartment, but it is not until later, when she gets the new tenant into her beautician's chair and relaxed by a manicure, that Betty starts talking.

Back in Minnesota after his first wife left him, Holits met and married Betty. Their life together began well enough, but then something happened. Holits bought a horse, took to betting on it, and gambled away the farm. Although Carver does not include the scene in this story, one need not imagine what passed between the travelers before their departure; Carver provides the prototype in "Vitamins":

> Then we got to talking about how we'd be better off if we moved to Arizona, someplace like that. I fixed us another one. I looked out the window. Arizona wasn't a bad idea. (*Where*, 187)

The idea occurs, distilled in the alembic of a mind beholding nothing. The character contemplates the prospect of departure, its unfulfilled promise, and symbolic escape. It is a familiar scene in Carver's fiction, and Carver leaves it out in "The Bridle."

Now in Arizona, their possessions reduced to an old station wagon, clothes, and a bridle, they are hoping for a change of luck and a new life. However, once again, something happens. Under the influence of drink and at the urging of others, Holits attempts to leap from the roof of the pool cabana into the water, misses, splits his head open, and is left permanently addled. Before long, the family gives up the apartment and moves on, leaving the bridle behind.

No doubt Holits had retained the tackle to flatter himself about his knowledge of horses, but by the time it is overlooked or left intentionally, the harness, reins, and bit have come to be, not an instrument Holits's uses to control and guide brute force, but rather the symbol of Holits's condition, controlled rather than controlling. As Marge puts it at the end of the story, "If you had to wear this thing between your teeth, I guess you'd catch on in a hurry. When you felt it pull, you'd know it was time. You'd know you were going somewhere."

One feels the power of that image, a negative force that life exercises on individuals, especially those on whom Carver focuses his attention. More often than not, they are incapable of stating with any precision what they sense. Consequently, we must interpret their strange physical reactions or indirect comments that say important things in commonplace utterances.

—Ewing Campbell, "Maturity: *Cathedral*," *Raymond Carver: A Study of the Short Fiction*. (New York: Twayne Publishers, 1992): pp. 48-70.

"What We Talk About When We Talk About Love"

"What We Talk About When We Talk About Love," the title story to one of Raymond Carver's most minimalistic short fiction collections, is a first person narrative told from the perspective of a character named Nick. Nick and his wife Laura are at Mel McGinnis and his wife Terri's house in Albuquerque and they are drinking gin. As they talk, they get on the subject of love. Mel talks about spiritual love and tells of how he spent five years at a seminary before quitting to go to medical school. Then Terri tells a story of her last boyfriend, Ed, whom she claims loved her so much that he wanted to kill her. She tells of a time when he dragged her by the ankles around their apartment, calling her a bitch and telling her that he loved her. Mel says that what Terri's talking about isn't love at all, but Terri insists that it was. Then Mel reveals that this same man had threatened to kill him.

Mel asks Nick and Laura whether they think what went on between Ed and Terri was love. They respond by saying that they would have to know more of the circumstances in order to judge, but that love can't be pinned down in one absolute way. Terri reveals that when she left Ed, he drank rat poison. It didn't kill him, but made his gums recede and turn black. So then he shot himself in the mouth, but this attempt was not initially successful either. Nick asks what went wrong with Ed's second attempt at suicide. Mel starts to answer by saying that he had shot himself with the twenty-two he had purchased for the sake of threatening them. Mel says that he had to get a gun of his own because of all the threats that Ed was making. He was also concerned about the late night calls to the hospital which he gets periodically.

Before the conversation goes too much further, Laura asks again what happened to Ed. Mel describes how the shot was heard by his neighbors who contacted the manager of their building, and Ed was rushed to the hospital. He lived for three days before he died. His head had ballooned to nearly three times its original size. Mel says that he and Terri fought over whether she should sit with Ed in his hospital room. Laura asks who won the fight and Terri answers by saying that she was with him when he died. Then Mel and Terri argue about whether this can be considered love. Terri admits that it's abnormal, but insists that it was indeed love. "'If that's love,'" Mel says, "'you can have it.'"

Laura declares that she and Nick know about love. Then she bumps her knee against her husband's leg and tells him that he's meant to respond. Nick explains how he made a dramatic scene out of kissing Laura's hand, which everyone found amusing. Terri asks them how long they've been together, and Laura blushes, saying that it's been nearly a year and a half. Terri jokes by suggesting that things might change over time. Mel passes the new bottle of gin around the table and they toast to love.

As the afternoon progresses, the group continues to drink gin and tell stories. Mel asks what anyone can really know about love. He mentions how he has difficulty accepting the fact that he had once loved his ex-wife, a woman for whom he holds nothing but ill feelings now. But he claims that at one time, he loved her as much as a person is capable. He relates the love he once held for his first wife with the love that Laura and Nick have for each other now. He speaks about how he and Terri had loved other people before, and suggests that Nick and Laura had also loved others before, both coming from past marriages just like Mel and Terri. This leads him to suggest that if anything ever happened to either him or Terri, they would grieve for the appropriate amount of time, but eventually love again, adding that this current love that they're experiencing would be little more than a memory. Mel's candor causes everyone to stop until the silence is broken by Terri who suggests that Mel is drunk.

When Mel goes into a another story about love, mild tension emerges between he and Terri. Mel persists with his new story, telling of a couple in their seventies who got into a car accident with a teenager who was killed instantly. The older couple was rushed to the hospital, alive but badly injured. Before he can finish his story, the conversation branches into another topic, about what one would do if they could choose a different path. Mel talks about his fantasy of being a knight in heavy armor. Nick claims that some knights suffocated inside their armor, or had heart attacks from the strain of wearing it.

As the conversation continues to circle, Laura asks Mel to finish his story about the injured elderly couple. He looks back at her and says that if he wasn't involved with Terri, and Nick wasn't his closest friend, he would fall in love with her. Terri tells him to finish his story so they can all go out to eat. Mel explains how he would visit this elderly couple everyday, noting their incredible progress. He explains how one day, after it was clear that they would both recover, the older man said he was horribly depressed. His depression was not over his condition, but that he couldn't turn his head and look at his wife. Mel repeats the conclusion several times, emphasizing that what was killing this man was that he couldn't look at her. "'Do you see what I'm saying?'" he asks the group who are unsure exactly how to respond.

As the group nears the end of their second bottle of gin, Mel says he wants to call his kids, asking if anyone would mind. Terri reminds him that his ex-wife might answer and that talking to her would make him feel even worse. Mel says he's in constant hope that his ex-wife will either get married to her boyfriend, whom Mel claims he is indirectly supporting, or die. He goes into how she's allergic to bees and he often hopes that she'll get stung. The story ends when the final bottle of gin is kicked, Mel spilling the remainder of his glass onto the table. The sun has almost set at this point, but no one dares to move, "not even when the room went dark."

"What We Talk About When We Talk About Love"

Mel McGinnis is a cardiologist and the first character the reader encounters. He and his second wife Terri are sharing gin and conversation with their friends Nick and Linda at their house in Albuquerque. When the conversation turns to the subject of love, Mel gets upset by Terri's suggestion that her ex-boyfriend, Ed, who tried to kill Terri and eventually killed himself, felt genuine love for her. As the evening progresses, Mel gets increasingly drunk and dominates the conversation, the focus of which remains on love.

Nick is the narrator of the story and a close friend of Mel McGinnis. He tells of how he made a dramatic scene of kissing Laura's hand.

Terri is the second wife of Mel McGinnis. When the conversation turns to the subject of love, Terri claims that her ex-boyfriend Ed loved her so much that he wanted to kill her. Mel takes exception to this and tension emerges between them.

Laura is Nick's second wife. She blushes at admitting her and Nick have been together for nearly a year and a half.

"What We Talk About When We Talk About Love"

MARSHALL BRUCE GENTRY AND WILLIAM L. STULL ON CARVER AS A MINIMALIST

[William L. Stull has been a professor of rhetoric at the University of Hartford. He has edited four books by Raymond Carver including *Those Days: Early Writings* and *No Heroics, Please,* and Marshall Bruce Gentry is an editor and critic who edited *Conversations with Raymond Carver.* In this excerpt, Gentry and Stull speak on the effect the minimalist label had on Carver following the publication of *What We Talk About When We Talk About Love.*]

No major interviews with Raymond Carver appear to have been conducted between 1979 and 1982, not even after *What We Talk About When We Talk About Love* received a glowing front-page notice in the *New York Times Book Review*. A longstanding tradition of critical disdain for the short story partially explains this inattention. A second factor prolonging the silence was the exhausting effort Carver had invested in the book. As he explained to Mona Simpson two years later, *What We Talk About* was the most "self-conscious" book he had ever written. "I pushed and pulled and worked with those stories before they went into the book to an extent I'd never done with any other stories," he said. In fact, some of the stories in the collection had been previously published in as many as three different versions, each more compressed and less explicit than the last. Taking his cue from Hemingway's theory of omission (and urge on in this practice by his longtime editor, Gordon Lish), Carver cut stories "to the marrow, not just to the bone" for What We Talk About Donald Newlove's capsule review suggests the outcome: "Seventeen tales of Hopelessville, its marriages and alcoholic wreckage, told in prose as sparingly clear as a fifth of iced Smirnoff."

What We Talk About won Carver accolades from Frank Kermode and others as "a full-grown master" of the storyteller's art. In addition, the bare-boned collection proved immensely influential on a younger generation of short-story writers coming of age in the 1980's Jayne Anne Phillips, for one, declared it "a book of fables for this decade." But the radical excisions had taken a toll on Carver's strength. For six months after *What We Talk About* went to press, he felt unable to write anything. Moreover, in retrospect he found the pared-down story texts aesthetically unsatisfying, especially after reviewers began dubbing him a literary "minimalist." The connotations of the word troubled him. "There's something about 'minimalist' that smacks of smallness of vision and execution that I don't like," he told Mona Simpson. Worse yet, the easy-to-apply label stuck to him. Interviewers and critics found it irresistible, and it was only years later, long after Carver had outgrown the "minimal" style of *What We Talk About*, that he was released from it. ("No minimalist he," chimed the *New York Times Book Review* editors when Where I'm Calling From, Carver's new and selected stories, appeared in 1988.)

—Marshall Bruce Gentry and William L. Stull, "Introduction," *Conversations with Raymond Carver*, eds. Marshall Bruce Gentry and William L. Stull (Jackson: University Press of Mississippi, 1990): pp. ix-xx.

NELSON HATHCOCK ON LANGUAGE

[Nelson Hathcock has been a professor of English at St. Xavier College in Chicago. He has published essays on James Dickey and Randell Jarrell, as well as a study on the fiction of Don DeLillo. In this excerpt, Hathcock discusses the language used in Carver's fiction.]

Language, Carver tells us, is both an obstacle and the means of confronting that obstacle. Even this passage is marked with the evidence of conflict: its indeterminacy gives evidence of the same malleability that Carver warns against. We cannot know how a word is "heavy" or "imprecise" or "inaccurate" or "blurred" without knowing a priori something of the author's intent. But such assumptions seem unnecessary if a corresponding "artistic sense" is brought into play because it is the re-written text—one produced by the reader—that is vital. Carver acknowledges the duplicity of words while asserting in the same breath that the writer fights against this liability, that emotions must be "bridled." He fights for, the implication seems to be, the vision of the reader. If the reader's eyes "slide right over" the "blurred" language, the reader does not in reality see it and so cannot re-vise it through his/her "artistic sense." For Carver then writing is reading and reading, writing. Both must be creative practices; in fact, both are the same practice. This observation is noteworthy because in "Feathers" and "Cathedral," the author allows characters to discover this "artistic sense" within themselves, and they begin to "read" for the first time.

An earlier story might serve as a counterpoint. "What We Talk About When We Talk About Love" speaks less of love than of the inadequacy of language to convey those monumental abstractions that spring from "unbridled emotions." Even the title suggests a practice of displacement. The attempt to talk about love results in story, but the stories in this case are struggles that fail to elicit their audience's "artistic sense." As Mel the cardiologist says, "I'll tell you what real love is . . . I mean, I'll give you a good example. And you can draw your own conclusions" (*What We Talk About,* 144). Like the writer posited by Carver above, Mel assumes that language must catalyze a process, but, as the story illustrates, he senses also the inadequacy of his role in that process. All his efforts to explain the meaning of his parables end in questions, non sequitur, or just inconclusive silence. We see the breakdown of response in Nick's final utterance: "I could hear my heart beating. I could hear everyone's heart. I could hear the human noise we sat there making, not one of us moving, not even when the room went dark" (154). This scene could be read as a moment of communion in which the story culminates, but for the presence of that "human noise." What better description of "blurred" language could Carver have settled upon? What more apt rendition of a scene in which "nothing will be achieved" than the stasis and darkness that blot out this story at its end, leaving literally nothing for the "eye" to rest upon?

In speaking of the self-conscious labor that went into the stories of *What We Talk About When We Talk About Love,* Carver resorts to the terminology of struggle:

I pushed and pulled and worked with those stories before they went into the book to an extent I'd never done with any other stories. When the book was put together and in the hands of my publisher, I didn't write anything at all for six months. And then the first story I wrote was "Cathedral," which I feel is totally different in conception and execution from any stories that have come before. . . . There was an opening up when I wrote that story. (*Fires* 204)

—Nelson Hathcock, "'The Possibility of Resurrection': Re-Vision in Carver's 'Feathers' and 'Cathedral,'" *Studies in Short Fiction*, Vol. 28, No. 1 (Winter, 1991): pp. 31-40.

MICHAEL TRUSSLER ON MINIMALISM

[Michael Trussler has been a lecturer at the University of Toronto, Erindale College. His criticism has been included in various journals as well as in *Critical Essays on Donald Barthelme.* In this excerpt, Trussler speaks on Carver's displeasure at the minimalist label that was pinned on him following the publication of *What We Talk About When We Talk About Love.*]

As was made abundantly clear in numerous interviews, Carver was antagonistic to being described as a "minimalist" writer. Viewing the term as a mere "tag," Carver believed that it was an unsatisfactory form of critical jargon, often serving to conflate dissimilar writers. Reluctant to accept the adequacy of the "appellation" in general, Carver specified that, if the label was to be used in connection to his own work, it should be reserved for his collection *What We Talk About When We Talk About Love (Conversations, 44)*. Numerous critics, while sympathetic to Carver's distaste for being neatly categorized, have focused on Carver's central tendency to rely on a poetics that practices Mies van der Rohe's dictum that "less is more." For Graham Clarke, Carver is "the quintessential minimalist, seemingly reducing to an absolute spareness both his subject matter and his treatment of it." Clarke's analysis cogently accentuates Carver's use of "silence":

The minimalism, as such, is based upon an absolute concern with the implications of a single mood: a space of habitation (and consciousness) where the syntax is as much concerned with the silent as it is with the spoken. (105)

Clarke's attention to the reciprocity in Carver's work (extending also to the reciprocity implicit in all literary minimalism) between the silent and the spoken provides a means of investigating not only Carver's narrative style, but the implications of such a style to our understanding of the short story's mechanics.

Carver's writing, as he himself acknowledged, owed much to Ernest Hemingway's celebrated "iceberg" aesthetic (seven-eighths of a narrative may take place beneath the surface of the text) and his frequently noted "theory of omission": "you could omit anything if you knew that [sic] you omitted and the omitted part would strengthen the story and make people feel something more than they understood" (Hemingway, 75). Hemingway's dependency upon ellipsis does considerably more than "make people feel something more than they understood"; it defamiliarizes both the signifier and the referent. Ihab Hassan writes that Hemingway distrusted "the accretions of language"; accordingly, his fiction (through its use of ellipsis, repetition and sparse, "ordinary" vocabulary) "creates itself in opposition, and style evolves into a pure anti-style" (88–89). Anti-style, for Hassan, as one of the hallmarks of postmodernism, is a recognition of literature's limitations; anti-style fractures textual unity and, demonstrating the power of "silence," it is "an intuition of the great emptiness behind the meticulous shape of things" (83). What is particularly important for an analysis of Carver's narrative style is Hassan's description of the "anti-languages" silence "creates":

> Some are utterly opaque, others completely transparent. These languages transform the presence of words into semantic absence and unloosen the grammar of consciousness. They accuse common speech. (13)

The significance of Hassan's observations to a discussion of Carver becomes immediately apparent when they are seen against the animosity of critics who believe that writers such as Carver are simply naively referential. Although many postmodernist critics disparage writers such as Carver, Charles Newman's diatribe against Neo-

Realism (a kingdom of which, according to Newman, Carver and Ann Beattie form the "aristocracy") is perhaps the most extreme in its vitriol: Neo-Realism is

> an artless analgesic worse than the addiction . . . . Against the mindless misappropriation of the metaphors of modern science [Newman does not approve of Thomas Pynchon], we get the concrete in the form of tennis shoes and the mandatory beer poured over the head . . . . Against the refusal to convince and represent, we get the self-evident which is never demonstrated. (93–94)

It is possible to view Carver's terse prose, with its seemingly transparent qualities (Newman's "tennis shoe") and elliptical style, as engaging considerably more than what is suggested in Newman's excessively denigrating polemic.

> —Michael Trussler, "The Narrowed Voice: Minimalism and Raymond Carver," *Studies in Short Fiction*, Vol. 31, No. 1 (Winter, 1994): pp. 23-38.

JON POWELL ON TENSION AND UNCERTAINTY

> [Jon Powell has taught English at the University of Southwestern Louisiana. In this excerpt, Powell talks about the role of uncertainty within the characters in the story.]

The tracing of changes in Raymond Carver's short story style is one of the most persistent topics of Carver criticism. Unfortunately, by focusing on change, critics have overlooked one of the most consistent aspects of Carver's short stories, their sense of menace. In *Fires*, Carver explains: "I like it when there is some sense of menace in short stories . . . . There has to be tension, a sense that something is imminent. . ." (17). William Stull notes that one of Carver's early stories, "Pastoral" (1963), is shaped "as an 'iceberg,' its marital conflict seven-eighths submerged" (*Raymond*, 466).

Throughout his career, Carver achieved a sense of menace by leaving out, or by providing only clues to, crucial aspects of the story. Both character and reader sense that something dangerous or menacing is "imminent" or "submerged," but both character and reader, unable to find the meaning of the given clues, must battle *between* readings of those clues. Menace develops as meaning itself becomes elusive. A second part of the method by which Carver achieves his unique sense of menace is his basing existential matters on the story's clues instead of on clearly stated facts.

In "What Is It?" the used-car salesman eyes Leo and "watches for sudden movement" (*Will You Please,* 216), watches for clues, and this watching highlights both characters' uncertainty about what the other sees or believes. This state of menacing uncertainty is equally evident in "What We Talk About When We Talk About Love" when the quiet conversation suddenly becomes much, much quieter. "'Just shut up for once in your life,' Mel said very quietly. 'Will you do me a favor and do that for a minute?'" (*What We Talk About,* 146) These sentences seem out of place in a conversation investigating love, so Mel's relationship to Terri is made ambiguous just when he is attempting to clarify it. Here, the first sentence is a harsh command, but the next is a request for a favor in the form of a question. The incongruity of tone confuses, contradicts, and, therefore, menaces.

However, again, this sense that language is confusing rather than clarifying and that unanswerable but crucial questions are being asked does not simply impart menace within Carver's stories. In stories taken from throughout his career, Carver's menace affects the reader as he or she struggles with the language that seems to be stating something quite simple, but that is in reality hiding something, something important, and something that, once it seems clear, still isn't an answer.

—Jon Powell, "The Stories of Raymond Carver: The Menace of Perpetual Uncertainty," *Studies in Short Fiction*, Vol. 31, No. 4 (Fall, 1994): pp. 647-656.

BRIAN STONEHILL ON THE ANECDOTES IN THE STORY

[Brian Stonehill is an essayist and a literary scholar whose criticism on Raymond Carver was published in the *Reference Guide to Short Fiction,* 1st ed. In this excerpt, Stonehill speaks on the anecdotes shared throughout the story.]

Intending to have a few drinks before going out to dinner, two married couples get caught up in conversation, and still haven't made it out the door by story's end. Such is the full extent of Raymond Carver's most celebrated story, "What We Talk about When We Talk about Love," first published in hardcover in 1981, running 17 pages. It was quickly termed "minimalist" by several critics, yet Carver himself rejected the label since it emphasizes the story's form to the neglect of its human focus.

Compared to the blue-collar inhabitants of Carver's fiction, the four characters—Mel McGinnis, his wife Terri, Nick, and his wife Laura—are relatively well-educated, but they share a sense of bafflement over matters of the heart. (Ironically, Mel, the most obtuse of the four, is even a cardiologist.) The more these characters talk about love, the less they feel they know, so that rather than moving towards understanding, they are eased by the growing darkness and the guzzled alcohol into nearly stupefied befuddlement. Yet witnessing the process leads the reader, remarkably, to genuine insight.

Two anecdotes serve the party as case studies. The first is summed up in a sentence that is key to Carver's style as well as to the story's themes: "Terri said the man she lived with before she lived with Mel loved her so much he tried to kill her." Both in its staccato rhythm of monosyllables, and in its insistent pattern of repetitiveness, the sentence (like the story's title) captures the barely-furnished nature of Carver's distinctive style. The paradoxical twinning of declarations of extreme love with a violent effort to kill the beloved is what gives Mel, in particular, an insoluble riddle that nonetheless prompts much of his increasingly boozy, angry, and hurt talk.

The second anecdote, related by Mel, concerns an elderly couple very badly injured in a car crash, whom Mel has attended in the hospital. Their greatest wish, as they lay all bandaged, was to be able to see each other, and this, too—like the report of a miracle—is something that Mel cannot understand, yet cannot dismiss.

Both couples eventually reveal themselves to the reader as pairs of refugees from previous failed marriages. True love has seemed, at one time, unattainable to them, and insulating themselves from vulnerability and pain has since become second nature. Yet they feel the tug of devotion as an amputee might miss a limb, and hence they are driven to talking, talking about and around love.

The story's title implies that, on this subject at least, either we don't mean what we say, or we don't say what we mean. Imprecision and inarticulateness are the joint curses of Carver's characters, and they are delineated precisely and articulately. In a 1981 essay entitled "On Writing," Carver embraced a saying of Ezra Pound's: "Fundamental accuracy of statement is the one sole morality of writing." He also expounded there his own formula for achieving the discipline of economy that is exemplified in "What We Talk About . . .": "Get in, get out. Don't linger. Go on." Yet the very redundancy of the title also shows how we bury its central concern beneath our own inarticulate words.

—Brian Stonehill, "'What We Talk About When We Talk About Love': Overview," *Reference Guide to Short Fiction*, 1st ed., ed. Noelle Watson, (St. James Press, 1994).

BILL MULLEN ON TELEVISUAL CULTURE IN THE SHORT STORIES OF RAYMOND CARVER

[Bill Mullen is an essayist and a scholar who has been involved in literary study at Youngstown State University. In this excerpt, Mullen speaks about the pared down prose in *What We Talk About When We Talk About Love*.]

Carver's stories, in apt comparison, are as transient and fleeting as commercials; they seem to click on and off with the abruptness of a channel change and gain power and force through accretion and repetition, in the manner of television's serial format. The stories seem consciously to pare down the reader's interaction time with characters as if to mimic the fragmentary experiences of people in his fiction or to mock the effect of consuming sound-bit-sized narratives. Indeed Carver's stories almost always eschew "cause and effect" exposition in favor of an arbitrary, jump-cut style reminiscent of channel-surfing with a remote control. The stories rarely provide "history" (background) or conclusions (a past or future sense); characters emerge like television beings—full-blown, past-less, without last names. Finally, Carver's characters constantly express the verbal impotence and exhaustion characteristic of the image-literate. Their words are as blunt as pictures, oversimplified and stripped of any vestige of personally resonant originality. Conversation is not only a lost art in Carver's fiction but a personal trauma; his characters seemingly suffer from a kind of mental or linguistic dyslexia in which sentences are incompletable, the right words never come to mind, or conversation takes place at cross-purposes, as if real communication were impossible. Indeed as many critics have noted, the very titles of Carver's stories suggest the desperate but awkward urgency of words (and lives) that circle around but never achieve full meaning, of experiences lived in the uncertain mode of rhetorical questions: "What We Talk About When We Talk About Love"; "Will You Please Be Quiet, Please?"; "One More Thing"; "Are You a Doctor?"; "What's in Alaska?"; "Why, Honey?"; "How About This?"; "What Is It?"

Carver's focus on blue-collar life was sharpest at the start of his career. Gradually, for a variety of reasons beyond the scope of this essay, that focus broadened to include less-restrictive subject matter and a more expansive and blatantly optimistic authorial tone. However, between Will You Please Be Quiet Please?; his first book, published in 1976, and Cathedral, published in 1984, Carver relentlessly documented the conditions of life in America's lower-middle- and working-class subcultures. I will focus on his most representative book, What We Talk About When We Talk About Love (1981), where the predominant theme and vision are of socially immobile, lower-middle- and working-class characters permanently deadened to their own condition by the dull hum and flicker of the tube, and where submission to an epistemology of failure—symbolized largely by television and its cousin technologies—is the distinctly postmodern fate of contemporary working-class Americans.

—Bill Mullen, "A Subtle Spectacle: Televisual Culture in the Short Stories of Raymond Carver," *Critique*, Vol. 39, Issue 2 (Winter, 1998): pp. 99-115.

WORKS BY

Raymond Carver

Near Klamath (poems). 1968.

Winter Insomnia (poems). 1970.

Put Yourself in My Shoes (chapbook). 1974.

Will You Please Be Quiet, Please? (stories). 1976.

At Night the Salmon Move (poems). 1976.

Furious Seasons and Other Stories. 1977.

What We Talk About When We Talk About Love (stories). 1980.

Cathedral (stories). 1983.

Fires: Essays, Poems, Stories. 1983.

If It Please You (poems). 1984.

Where Water Comes Together with Other Water (poems). 1985.

This Water (poems). 1985.

Dostoevsky: A Screenplay (with Tess Gallagher). 1985.

The Stories of Raymond Carver. 1985.

Ultramarine (poems). 1986.

Where I'm Calling From (stories). 1988.

A New Path to the Waterfall (poems). 1989.

No Heroics, Please: Uncollected Writings (published posthumously). 1992.

Short Cuts (stories published posthumously). 1993.

Raymond Carver

Abrams, Linsey. "A Maximalist Novelist Looks at Some Minimalist Fiction." *Mississippi Review* 40/41 (Winter 1985): 24-30.

Adelman, Bob. *Carver Country: The World of Raymond Carver.* Introduction by Tess Gallagher. New York: Charles Scribner's Sons, 1990.

Applefield, David. "Fiction and America: Raymond." *International Journal of Contemporary Writing and Art* 8-9 (1987-88): 6-15.

Atlas, James. "Less Is Less." *Atlantic Monthly*, June 1981. 96-98.

Bakhtin, M.M. *The Dialogic Imagination.* Trans. Caryl Emerson and Michael Holquist. Austin: University of Texas Press, 1953.

Banks, Russell. "Raymond Carver: Our Stephen Crane." *Atlantic* 268.2 (August 1991): 99-103.

Barth, John. "A Few Words about Minimalism." *New York Times Book Review*, 28 December 1986, 1-2, 25.

Barthelme, Frederick. "On Being Wrong: Convicted Minimalist Spills Bean." *New York Times Book Review,* April 3, 1988.

Beattie, Ann. "Carver's Furious Seasons." *Canto* 2.2 (Summer 1978): 178-82.

Bugeja, Michael J. "Tarnish and Silver: An Analysis of Carver's *Cathedral.*" *South Dakota Review* 24, no. 3 (1986): 73-87.

Campbell, Ewing. *Raymond Carver: A Study of the Short Fiction.* New York: Twayne, 1992.

Carpenter, David. "What We Talk About When We Talk About Carver." *Descant* [Toronto] 56/57 (Spring-Summer 1987): 20-43.

Clark, Tom. "Raymond Carver's Final Chapter." *San Francisco Times Book Review*, July 2, 1989: 3.

Clarke, Graham. "Investing the Glimpse: Raymond Carver and the Syntax of Silence." *The New American Writing: Essays on American Literature Since 1970.* New York: St. Martin's Press, 1990. 99-122.

Cushman, Keith. "Blind, Intertextual Love: 'The Blind Man' and Raymond Carver's '*Cathedral.*'" *Etudes Lawrenciennes* 3 *(1988): 125-38.*

Day, R.C. "Raymond Carver: A Remembrance." *Toyon* 35 (Spring 1989): 20.

Dunn, Robert. "Fiction That Shrinks from Life." *New York Times Book Review,* 30 June 1985, 1, 24-25.

Edwards, Thomas R. "The Short View: *Will You Please Be Quiet, Please?*" *New York Review of Books*, 1 April 1976, 35-36.

Gentry, Marshall Bruce, and William L. Stull, eds. *Conversations with Raymond Carver*. Jackson: University of Mississippi Press, 1990.

Halpert, Sam. *Raymond Carver: An Oral Biography* (interviews). Iowa City: University of Iowa Press, 1995.

Jenks, Tom. "Together in Carver Country." *Vanity Fair,* 49.10 (October 1986): 114.

Kaufmann, David. "Yuppie Postmodernism." *Arizona Quarterly*, 47.2 (Summer, 1991): 93-116.

Lopez, Ken. *Raymond Carver: A Collection (descriptive catalog)*. Hadley: Ken Lopez Books, 1993.

Meyer, Adam. "Now You See Him, Now You Don't, Now You Do Again: The Evolution of Raymond Carver's Minimalism," *Critique* 30.4 (Summer 1989): 239-51.

———. *Raymond Carver*. New York: Twayne, 1995.

Moffett, Penelope. "Raymond Carver," *Publishers Weekly, (*27 May, 1988): 42-44.

Nesset, Kirk. *The Stories of Raymond Carver: A Critical Study*. Athens: Ohio University Press, 1995.

Newlove, Donald. "What We Talk About When We Talk About Carver." *Saturday Review*, April, 1981: 77.

O'Connell, Shaun. "Carver's Fires Burn with Magic." *Boston Globe*, (17 July, 1983): sec. A, 55-56.

Pope, Dan. "The Post-Minimalist American Story or What Comes After Carver?" *Gettysburg Review* 1, no. 2 (1988): 332.

Queenan, Joe. "Character Assassins," *American Spectator* 21 (December, 1988): 14–16.

Runyon, Randolph Paul. *Reading Raymond Carver*. Syracuse: Syracuse University Press, 1992.

Saltzman, Arthur M. *Understanding Raymond Carver*. Columbia: University of South Carolina Press, 1988.

Skenazy, Paul. "Life in Limbo: Ray Carver's Fiction." *Enclitic* 11, no. 1 (1988): 77-83.

Stull, William L. And Maureen P. Carroll, eds. *Remembering Ray: A Composite Biography of Raymond Carver* (interviews). Santa Barbara: Capra, 1993.

VanderWeele, Michael. "Raymond Carver and the Language of Desire," *Denver Quarterly* 22, no. 1 (1987): 108-22.

Weber, Bruce. "Raymond Carver: A Chronicler of Blue-Collar Despair." *New York Times Magazine*, 24 June 1984, 36-38, 42-46, 48-50.

Wolff, Tobias. "Raymond Carver: Had His Cake and Ate It Too," *Esquire*, (September, 1989): 240-48.

ACKNOWLEDGMENTS

Critique: Studies in Contemporary Fiction, Vol. 30, No. 4, pp.239-240, Summer 1989. Reprinted with permission of the Helen Dwight Reid Educational Foundation. Published by Heldref Publications, 1319 Eighteenth St., NW, Washington, DC 20036-1802. Copyright © 1989.

"Narration and Interiority in Raymond Carver's 'Where I'm Calling From'" by Claudine Verley © 1989 from Journal of the Short Story in English, No.13 by University Press of Angers. Reprinted by Permission.

"'Where I'm Calling From': A Textual and Critical Study" by Thomas J. Haslam © 1992 from *Studies in Short Fiction,* Vol. 29, No.1 by Newberry College. Reprinted by Permission.

"Narration and Interiority in Raymond Carver's 'Where I am Calling From'" by Kirk Nesset © 1995 from *The Stories of Raymond Carver: A Critical Study* by Ohio University Press. Reprinted with the permission of Ohio University Press/ Swallow Press, Athens, Ohio.

"Grown Men in 'Where I'm Calling From'" by Michael Sonkowsky © 1998 from *Short Stories for Students,* Vol. 3 by Gale Group. Reprinted by Permission.

"Stories of Loneliness" by Irving Howe © 1983 from *The New York Times Book Review* by The New York Times Agency. Reprinted by Permission.

"'The Calm' 'A Small Good Thing,' and 'Cathedral': Raymond Carver and the Discovery of Human Worth" by Mark A.R. Facknitz © 1986 from *Studies in Short Fiction*, Vol. 23, No.3 by Newberry College. Reprinted by Permission.

Critique: Studies in Contemporary Fiction Vol. 31, No. 2, Winter 1990, pp. 125-136. Reprinted with permission of the Helen Dwight Reid Educational Foundation. Published by Heldref Publications, 1319 Eighteenth St., NW, Washington, DC 20036-1802. Copyright © 1990.

"Carver County" by Tess Gallagher © 1990 from *Carver County* by Charles Scribner's Sons. Reprinted by Permission.

INDEX OF
Themes and Ideas